Deal Me In!

101 Columns the Casino Operators
Don't Want You to Read

Mark Pilarski

Winners Publishing
774 Mays Blvd. Suite 10
Incline Village, NV 89451

Deal Me In

ISBN: 0-9653214-2-8

Address all inquires to the publisher:

Winners Publishing
774 Mays Blvd. Suite 10
Incline Village, NV 89451
(231) 929-2740

Printed and bound in the United States of America

10 9 8 7 6 5 4 3

Photo credits:
Front cover: PhotoDisc

The material contained in this book is intended to inform and educate the
reader and in no way represents an inducement to gamble legally or illegally.

Dedication

To my beautiful wife Renee and my talented son Nicholas. Two natural winners in the game of life.

Acknowledgements

I would like to express my sincere thanks to my editor, Colleen O'Brien. Colleen allowed me to see the forest while she concentrated on pruning the trees. Thank you, Colleen, for translating my book from Pilarski to English, my dashes and slashes from hieroglyphics to elements of style.

The loyal readers of *Deal Me In.* It is through their questions and their letters of thanks for teaching them to be winners that makes writing this column worthwhile.

Thanks once again to my wife Renee, who makes me deal an honest game.

Preface

With the explosion of casino gambling in North America–operating in 32 states–gambling entertainment is becoming a cannibal enterprise of Wal-Martian proportions. What better way to preface this book than by letting a casino soothsayer, with his set of talking points, tell you the way it really is.

"The slot machine entertainment business targets everybody. Money's money. What's the difference if it's a social security check, a welfare check, a stock dividend check?" "When we put 50 machines in, I always consider them 50 more mousetraps. You have to do something to catch a mouse." "It's our duty to extract as much money from the customers as we can and send them home with a smile on their face." – BOB STUPAK, CASINO OWNER

After reflecting on Stupak's words, do you really think you stand a chance against the Lords of Chance? If you are one of the uneducated 95% making your "contribution" to the neon arcade, you'll end up one way—a casino fatality. But if everyone who gambled followed the guidelines in this book, every casino would be forced to close its doors. Better yet, follow this one golden nugget of advice; *Only make casino bets that have a house advantage of two percent or less,* Las Vegas, Atlantic City and every saw dust joint in between would be boarded up in six months.

This is why casino operators don't want you to read this book. They would much prefer uneducated players making dumb wagers, bets that have a house edge higher than the interest you pay on your Visa card.

Can I prove beyond a reasonable doubt that casino operators much prefer the Tootsie-Pop crowd, known as "a sucker's born every minute" club? Yep! Go into a casino and try counting cards at blackjack. Casino operators will immediately stop your play dead in its tracks. They simply don't want you to use any of your God-given gray matter, not even for the simplest advantage against the house. Absurd as it sounds, that's the truth of it.

It is finally time for you to let somebody else pay the light bills. It's time for you to learn to beat the odds. If you are going to gamble, you should be as well informed as possible. *Deal Me In* will give you all information necessary to enable you to make the best bets and play the best strategies. Instead of playing against the odds, you'll play like a winner. Only by learning the insider tricks can you come out dollars ahead.

You will learn from hundreds of mistakes that my readers have made, from gamblers who desperately needed help. I'll show you, question by question, the most important gambling principles you need to know. You will be armed with tips that will immediately strengthen your gambling prowess. And that, my friends, is what my columns have always been about—educating the player and playing to win. So with great pleasure I invite you to join in the conversation.

One final note. Over the past few years I have received numerous letters from readers who do not gamble at all. One editor of a newspaper who carries *Deal Me In* told me that half of his correspondence from readership have never set foot in a casino. They enjoy the column for the insider information—for my sins I spent my 18-year penance working in these grind joints—and because all gambling questions, whether technical, societal, philosophical or what's my favorite buffet in Las Vegas, are open to discussion in my Q&A forum.

So occasionally I will answer questions on the lottery, sweepstakes, bingo, kitchen table poker, even carnival games of chance. As long as it's your hard-earned money at risk, no question, on any form of gambling, is trivial to me.

Mark Pilarski

♠ 1 ♠
Just Say NO to Keno

DEAR MARK: *Though I'm not a keno player, my favorite casino offers a Special Bonus Keno ticket. All I have to do is hit 19 out of 20, and I win $250,000. Is this ticket worth a try?* **Marti S.**

The nerve of your favorite casino calling it a "Special Bonus" ticket. Let me illustrate how appalling this ticket is. Let's say you were to play one keno ticket per second, 24 hours a day, 365 days a year. According to laws of probability you will catch 19 out of 20 once every 93,420,116 years. What are the odds of hitting it? Two quadrillion, 946 trillion, 096 billion, 780 million to one.

Unfortunately, Marti, this isn't the only ruthless ticket in keno. The chances of hitting 10 of 10—and mind you they will only pay you $50,000—is nine times harder than hitting your state lottery. Then the casino has the audacity to pay you what is called an "aggregate payoff," meaning if both you and someone else are playing the same numbers and it hits solid, you split the money.

Or how about this popular ticket here in Nevada—the 15 spot. Chances of your hitting it? 428 billion to one. Tall odds, but consider that no person has ever hit a solid 15 spot, a solid 14 spot, a solid 13 and to the best of my knowledge, a 12 out of 12.

As you can see, Marti, these long-shot tickets—or keno in general for that matter—are a game designed for the Tootsie-Pop crowd; known by the casinos as "a sucker's born every minute" club.

DEAR MARK: *My husband claims that certain casinos use different weighted dollar coins for their slots in order to make it sound as if people are winning in the casino. Is he right?* **Sally L.**

Your husband is on to the casinos. It's not heavier coins, though, but the tray where the coins fall. Casino operators have long understood the value of "the sounds of winning," so what some do is install "loud drop bowls," which are the metal trays that catch the slugs when your slot is paying off. These deeper pans tend to make more noise when the coins drop, creating the misimpression that people are winning big.

Unfortunately, that sense of luck is really nothing more than an illusion the casino hopes will stir interest in playing their machines.

DEAR MARK: *How Did the strip get its name?* **Suzanne S.**

One day I was walking down the strip in Las Vegas and overheard a couple vehemently arguing over how "The Strip" got it's name. The husband said; "Bugsy Siegel named it when he built the Flamingo—and I should know, I played there the second week it was open." The wife believed it was Liberace who named the Strip.

The dialog was hideous and I would have butted in, but like I said, they were arguing, actually screaming at a level that brought security out of Caesar's Palace. Now, I've seen some skirmishes over positioning in a $3.49 prime rib buffet line, but over how the Strip was named? It's a first.

So, Suzanne, here's how "The Strip" got it's name.

Known also as Las Vegas Boulevard and earlier the Los Angeles Highway, The Strip's name came from a Los Angeles Police Captain named Guy McAfee, who said it reminded him of Sunset Boulevard (Strip) in LA. The story doesn't end there with Captain McAffe. He was a Las Vegas casino owner as well. McAfee purchased the Pair-O-Dice on the Los Angeles Highway in 1938 and reopened it as the 91 Club.

Liberace's early fame came from being the first to demand, and get, $50,000 a week to perform in Vegas.

"In the case of an earthquake hitting Las Vegas, be sure to go straight to the keno lounge. Nothing ever gets hit there."
– AN ANONYMOUS CASINO BOSS

♠ 2 ♠
Do Two-Year-Olds Gamble? You Bet!

DEAR MARK: *Do you think that kids who play arcade video games are being pre-programmed to gamble since the slot machines of today are video based?* **Ronnie M.**

Forget video games, Ronnie, I can prove to you that two-year-olds gamble. Strong statement, yes, but no whiff of bologna.

First, let me give you two examples of children gambling casino style. On the Boardwalk in Atlantic City children can freely walk into an arcade and play true slot machines by exchanging quarters for tokens. They win crummy prizes in exchange for the tickets the slot spits out. Another example is at the children's arcade at the Circus Circus in Reno. A child can play Flip It, the casino game that flips quarters into the air and on rare occasion pushes them down into trays. They disguised it in name only by calling it Jungle Jamboree. Again, kids get to exchange tickets for worthless prizes.

But I did say two-year-olds. To prove I have one foot planted in mid-air, how about the two-year-old who makes a path with Linus blanket in hand to that thingamajig at the supermarket door that dispenses those plastic transparent eggs. For a quarter a young tot can win an egg containing a bracelet, a cheap watch, but most likely a 3¢ ring—more on that below. These vending machines are classic slot machines.

So is it true gambling? Absolutely. Courts have found that every gambling apparatus must consist of three components; consideration, chance and prize. The child pays something of value (consideration) to use the vending machine: if he wins he receives something of value (prize), usually less than the amount bet; and the outcome depends on chance. Because all three elements are present on the vending machines that dispenses these plastic eggs, this would be considered a true gambling device.

Granted, I doubt anyone would arrest or even put the kibosh on a child for playing grocery store slots, but I do wonder why these vending operators have gone uncontested for so long. Who owns these cash cows milking kids out of quarters?

By the way, Ronnie, vis-à-vis some insider information, the cost of those plastic egg prizes produced in Asia is about 3¢, and there is only one true prize (junky watch) per two hundred eggs. Our offspring are up against tougher odds than the tightest one-armed bandit.

The stimulation to gamble does begin early for many children, well before an arcade adventure. And what parent in his or her right mind is really going to say no? We have to be quarter generous to our kids. They will be choosing our nursing home.

DEAR MARK: *When casino executives mention both the "handle" and "hold" of a slot machine, what do they mean?* **Al R.**

The "handle" is the total amount of all coins played through a slot machine. The "hold" (also called "win") is the amount the casino held as profit. The "yield" is the casino's win expressed as a percentage of the profit.

DEAR MARK: *Every week I enter all kinds of contests. To this day the telephone has not rung to acknowledge that I'm a winner. Do you think the phone will ever ring?* **Russell G.**

According to Roxy Roxborough, czar of the Las Vegas handicappers, "Your chances are a million to one that any one telephone call will be financially rewarding. Compare that against the caller being a telemarketer or an undesirable in-law, three to one."

Your best bet, Russell, is to leave the answering machine on.

♠ 3 ♠
The Potential for Abuse Great

DEAR MARK: *I just started playing around on the internet and found that I can gamble from my home in Tennessee. How safe is this?* **Chuck K.**

For better or worse, cyberspace is gambling's next frontier, and many experts are calling it "the real killer application on the internet." Personally, I think home computers and gambling are a frightening combination, and I would advise you, Chuck, not to participate in this unregulated venture.

Let's first start with the legality of it. According to the FBI, IRS, Justice Department and numerous state attorney generals, internet gamblers are breaking the law when using a desktop computer as a gambling terminal. Additionally, U.S. laws, including the Interstate Wire Act, prohibit anyone in the gambling business from taking bets over a network—including the internet—that crosses state and international borders.

Next, expect big risks when opening an account with your credit card or using digital cash that establishes a direct link to your checking account from someone you have never met. Most of these on-line gambling establishments are shadow companies with headquarters offshore. Reason? To take advantage of lax regulation abroad and, of course, to distance themselves from U.S. law enforcement officials. And who are these people running digital casinos? One of the larger operators is a ninth-grade dropout from Toronto who bills himself as "the Bugsy Siegel of the internet." He got his startup capital running 900-number services such as Dial-a-Psychic. For some reason, I've got a bad feeling about sending him my credit card number.

Finally, Chuck, you have to ask yourself questions about the games themselves. How do you really know whether their casino system is secure, or if you are being cheated? What's to stop a virtual casino from fixing the order of numbers coming up on a virtual crap game? They could put a secret algorithm in their program to roll more sevens when the house gets behind. Or how about a hacker who discovers a flaw in the software and starts depositing winnings to his account, essentially stealing the payouts from the true winners?

Here's the bottom line: Chuck, I can't advise anyone to wire money thousands of miles away to an unregulated, uncontrolled and probably illegal enterprise, give them a credit card number, then trust them to tell me when I've won. Sorry, but there is something wrong with this picture!

DEAR MARK: *I realize this question might be hard to answer in this setting (your column), but what is the exact pronunciation of Baccarat?* **Susan D.**

My first inclination was to suggest you to look it up in a dictionary, but far to many players mispronounce baccarat. The "t" in baccarat is silent and correctly pronounced it's ba-ka-ra, not back-a-rat (a small rodent found nibbling on buffet leftovers).

DEAR MARK: *Deuces Wild is my favorite video poker game. The casino where I normally play offers only a four coin return for four-of-a-kind. You suggest finding a machine that returns five coins for four-of-a-kind. How much more of an edge am I giving the casino?* **Grant S.**

Plenty! Try six percent. With maximum coin play and perfect strategy, a five-coin return for four-of-a-kind gives you a slight edge against the house—a 100.76% return versus 94.34% if the machine returns just four coins.

DEAR MARK: *I was reading one of your columns in which you mentioned 'scared money'. I'm new to gambling and wondered what this term means.* **A. A.**

It's June 1 and your rent is due. With insufficient capital to pay your landlord, you decide to gamble, erroneously believing you can chase down luck. That's scared money! Which leads me to give any gambler this sagacious advice: Only bet what you can afford to lose. Money for rent, car payments or any of life's necessities has no place in a casino.

♠ 4 ♠
Gambler's Ruin

DEAR MARK: *Casino Windsor has high table minimums and low table maximums. Is this a player advantage?* **Danny B.**

Quite the contrary, Danny. It's a huge advantage for the casino, and here's why. Casinos win for two reasons. First, a statistical edge (percentage advantage) on each and every game, and second, they have a whole lot more cash and staying power than you do. For the latter, it's a simple concept called "gambler's ruin." In essence, it's how long will it take you—with your limited bankroll—to lose everything to a casino, which has a relatively infinite wad of cash. So even if you do have a short-term winning streak, Danny, when the house has this infinite stake, they can, and will, always outlast you.

Now to your situation playing the high minimums/low maximums limits. When you have a casino with a competition-free monopoly, you tend to find table limits that, in my humble opinion, border on larceny. This scenario eliminates low-stakes betting (high minimums); plus, the ability to parlay your winnings by increasing your bets (low maximums) is removed. Unfortunately, when you play under these conditions, depletion of a low roller's bankroll in a matter of minutes is not uncommon.

So the long and short of it is this, Danny. Avoid playing high minimums/low maximums table limits like the plague!

DEAR MARK: *If I were to hit $1 million on a progressive quarter slot machine, will they pay me all at once?* **Dave G.**

Forget borrowing Uncle Fred's three-quarter-ton pickup truck to haul off 42,000 pounds of quarters. Look at the machine closely, Dave.

7

A sign placed inconspicuously on the machine will read something like "Progressive Jackpot paid in 25 equal installments. First installment paid upon validation of win."

One exception is a statewide progressive machine in Nevada, and other locations, called "Cool Millions." Bet 3 bucks, line up 3 ducks, and you win "the first million" instantly. Now if you get your ducks in line, Dave, make them pay you in $100 bills. They will weigh only twenty and a half pounds.

DEAR MARK: *How come I always lose when I'm drinking with my buddies vs. sober and winning by myself?* **Brad S.**

Casinos are fundamentally democratic institutions where all are welcome, united in the brotherhood (and sisterhood) of losing. Free drinks (chip remover) which have always been part of the casino ambience, speed up the process. Then there's Brad, gambling with friends, raised testosterone, elevated male bravado and sipping hooch, not for pleasure but gulping for effect. What do you expect, Brad? I'll tell you: the demise of a normally sensible gambler!

All bets are off on the quality of your play, Brad, when influenced by any intoxicating beverage.

DEAR MARK: *I witnessed something amusing recently in a casino, someone sprinkling salt all over a slot machine. Did she really think this would bring her luck?* **Edith C.**

By sprinkling salt, this superstitious gambler was trying to make the machine pay off by using salt's association with money. It comes from ancient times when workers were paid with salt, called "salarium." We know that word today as salary.

Now my own personal feelings about (a) luck and (b) superstition. When it comes to the goddess "Lady Luck," I'm an atheist. Only smart wagers will bring you luck. Salt to me has more value disguising my own cooking, not showering a machine with it.

"The smarter you play, the luckier you'll be."
– MARK PILARSKI

♠ 5 ♠
Good Advice Can Come From Anywhere

DEAR MARK: *I very much enjoy your helpful hints on casino gambling in your columns, but I'm curious, what's the best advice you've ever heard preached?* **Ned C.**

In the casino business, the best admonition to get ahead is "Never make suggestions." As for a gambling nugget, the following voice of reason caught my attention while I was walking down the Strip in Las Vegas.

A panhandler approached and asked if I had any loose change so he could buy a hot dog. Unfortunately, spare change doesn't exist in Las Vegas. Strategically positioned slot machines allow you to travel light. But I guess I'm an easy mark for a hot dog story so I gave him a nickel chip—casino talk for $5—that I had in my coat pocket.

After his gratitude for my allowing him to bump up into buffet dining, or whatever, he shared some of his best gaming wisdom. "Go downtown to Binion's and make a pass line bet and take those 10 times odds. It's one of the best bets in the house," he said.

Guess what, Ned? He's right on. The house advantage on this wager is .018%. Those multiple odds he was talking about— zero casino advantage. It's the line bet where the casino enjoys its slight edge. And I mean slight. Expected mathematical loss on a $1 line bet with $10 odds, about 4¢. But we can combat that too, Ned. Throw in a few free drinks and pry a breakfast out of a floorman, you're getting to the point where they're paying you to play.

Yes, advice comes from the funniest places.

DEAR MARK: *Are the dice placed on the crap game ever inspected for imperfections so the same number won't repeat itself?* **Steve B.**

Because I can predict with 100% certainty that every casino has at least one lazy pit boss—I was one—you can be assured that the dice placed on the game are near perfect. The perks for this idle behavior? Going up to the boss's office and inspecting dice. This meant feet on the head honcho's desk, Oprah on the tube and talking on the phone long distance to friends and family because I knew the secret dial code. Oh, and inspecting dice with a micrometer to make sure our dice were produced to a tolerance level of .0005 of an inch.

But we were the second line of defense. Dice makers who cut this poly-sorbate plastic in lots of five or six deal in tolerances of .0002, with imperfections discarded, making the random nature of a dice throw a certainty.

By the way, Steve, no not you, Steve, my former boss Steve. You never asked, but those long distance calls to Michigan were probably mine.

DEAR MARK: *On a trip to Las Vegas, I tracked each and every hand (see enclosed) that I won and lost. As you can see I lost more hands (160 losses, 142 wins) than I won. How can you write in your column that when playing blackjack the house edge is less than 1% when you lose more often than win?* **Jon G.**

Throw your chart away, Jon. Blackjack is a horrible game if your foundation for winning is based on how many hands you actually win.

Excluding ties, a player loses approximately 53% of all hands. However, the casino, bless their hearts, permits you to double down and split hands after viewing the dealer up card. This allows the player to get more money in the circle when conditions are favorable. In addition, they give you that sweet 3 to 2 payoff for a blackjack.

That is why, Jon, the casino has only a half percent edge over the disciplined basic strategy player.

♠ 6 ♠
The Good, the Bad and the Ugly

DEAR MARK: *All casinos have slot machines, blackjack tables, etc. Is there a difference between casino A, B and C?* **Michelle R.**

PLENTY, Michelle! My goal as a player-advocate columnist is to develop players who can identify beneficial gaming situations, not only the bets you make in a casino but the casinos themselves. So are all casinos the same? No, no—the correct answer is this: No two casinos are alike. Some are good, and some, well let me describe the differences:

The Good: Though more come to mind, I'll give you two examples: the Club Cal Neva in Reno and Binion's Horseshoe in Las Vegas. Here's what they offer their cherished players—that's you and me, Michelle. Besides some of the cheapest food prices—99¢ breakfasts and $3.99 steak dinners—they offer great gaming plays like 25¢ crap games with up to 10 times odds, single-deck blackjack with liberal rules, single-zero roulette, excellent video poker pay tables, loads of loose nickel and quarter machines and comps just for breathing.

These casinos, the ones that treat you like a treasured commodity and are always trying to increase buyer value, are casinos I hope you, Michelle, will migrate to.

The Bad: Quite possibly, this is the casino you normally play in. Gouging table limits on the weekends; tough getting comps (stale popcorn and lucky dogs don't cut it); poor pay tables on video poker machines; and tight slots. Basically, they put out games for your convenience and count their money. Plus, the practice of my #1 rule of casino management—who's the boss, you the customer—is limited. If your favorite casino has any of the above symptoms, maybe it's time to change.

11

The Ugly: Casino Windsor. Knowing full well they have the only game in town, Detroiters who cross the river to Canada—and all players for that matter—are being ripped off, big time! For starters, charging $40 for valet parking and instant admission versus parking two blocks away and waiting up to two hours to get in is absurd. Hopefully that has changed.

But I'm just warming up. They opened with $15 table minimums/ $200 maximums—which can deplete a modest bankroll in mere minutes; zero nickel, very limited quarter and mostly dollar slots; and very poor pay tables on video poker machines equaling what you would find in airports and grocery stores. Finally the triple whammy: I found food service at the buffet slow, quality only fair, and prices high. Unequivocally, two thumbs down on Casino Windsor.

But even I get the worst of it once in a while, Michelle. After spending the day lounging poolside at the Mirage Hotel/Casino in Las Vegas, my friends and I decided instead of watching a sporting event in their sports book—we were just too tired (lazy) to leave the room—that some beer and a few snacks in our room would do the trick. We each threw in a few bucks and sent our runner (me, scissors cuts paper) down to a convenience store called "Impulse" in the Mirage Hotel. Noting here that all the "buyer impulse" merchandise we purchased wasn't priced, the cost of two six-packs, one small package of Jerky, and two eight-ounce boxes of Cheese Nips: $29.43! Thought I would pass along my lesson learned to you.

So, Michelle, the key here is shopping for value, not only on your bet selection, but learning to shop casinos. Warren Nelson, owner of the Club Cal Neva in Reno, has lived by a simple principle most of his career: "Give the players the best bet (lowest odds for the house) that you can while still making a profit, and they will play longer, leave satisfied and come back bringing their friends." I applaud his sound reasoning and, Michelle, that's the kind of casino where you should play.

The Wampanoag Tribe has a machine, and they say, "It's completely idiot proof." I told them they've got it all wrong. I want a machine that is "idiot friendly."
– Former Massachusetts Governor William F. Weld

♠ 7 ♠

Bankroll Meltdown is Inevitable

DEAR MARK: *Over the past 20 years I have found great pleasure in making my monthly trip to Atlantic City. My bankroll is limited to $200 and I generally stick with most of the low house percentage bets that you recommend in your column. Sometimes I break even, win every third or fourth time, or lose it all. My question is, will I ever become a "consistent winner" before I join the Angels in a crap game? I'm looking for divine intervention.* **Sandy G.**

There is no real easy way to break this to you so I'll get right to the point: NO!

Though every dog has his day, don't expect a good week. It's not because you're making the wrong bets, nor playing smart, not even because you're not a decent, hard-working person worth more than an occasional bone tossed your way by the casino. You lack the essential component necessary to whip the casino, and no celestial spirit can help.

And that, my friend, is a big-time bankroll. Why? Because the casino has a whole lot more cash and staying power than you do. In the industry we call it "gambler's ruin." In essence, it's how long will it take you—with your limited bankroll—to lose everything to a casino, which has a relatively infinite vault of money.

You come to the casino armed with X amount of dollars, and the casino has the treasures of Rome. It is the ultimate secret weapon the casino possesses. So even if you do have a short-term winning streak, when the house has this infinite stake, they can, and will, outlast you.

13

Test this truism out yourself. Sit at your kitchen table and play an even-up game like War with an opponent. You start off with $50 worth of monopoly money, and your adversary—we'll call him Joe Casino—begins play with $50,000. Now start playing at $5 a hand and you will immediately note some normal fluctuations inherent to gambling— like you winning six or seven hands in a row. But without fail, a losing streak will appear and your bankroll will start to deteriorate. You'll quickly notice that your modest bankroll cannot weather the bad streaks that eventually come your way.

The casino can, and will, grind away at your wad of cash because their bankroll is enormous in comparison to your bets. Before long you're out of cash. A casino fatality Armageddon style.

So the lesson here is that not even an archangel will help you become a "consistent winner." Only a Catholic Church size bankroll can.

DEAR MARK: *I was on a crap game for the first time and asked the dealer what the difference was between a hard 8 and a regular 8. She politely told me the difference when another player started yelling at me because I was holding up the game. Talk about being embarrassed. What did I do wrong?* **Meg B.**

Nothing! There is never a need to be embarrassed, Meg. You are to be applauded for asking for help. All too many players try to cover up their shortcomings and waste their hard-earned money playing casino games they know little about.

So no question, Meg, regarding gambling is "dumb." Well, that's not quite true. I was dealing blackjack late one evening in downtown Reno when a man approached me and asked: "Where are the slot machines for kids?" That was dumb. No, pathetic.

"The race is not to the swift, nor the battle to the strong, but that's the way to bet." – GRANTLAND RICE

♠ 8 ♠
The Classic Roman Myth Approach to Gambling

DEAR MARK: *I'm about to make my first trip to Las Vegas. Can you give me your favorite King Midas tip that will turn my trip into gold?* **Jerome S.**

Why King Midas, Jerome? When I think of King Midas my thoughts turn toward greed. In Ovid's Greek tale, Midas was so greedy he wanted everything he touched to turn to gold. To his delight, his wish came true, and he proceeded to gild everything in sight. But like a rapacious player who wants to win every hand, his fate was tragic in the end. He killed his own beloved daughter with his magical touch.

But you probably don't give a hoot about some Roman poet's tale and only want a hot tip for success, so here's my favorite: Only make bets that have less than a two percent house advantage.

You didn't mention what type of casino games you prefer, Jerome, so I'll trumpet my favored plays below. All represent wagers that have a house edge of less than two percent.

Blackjack: With perfect basic strategy.
Video Poker: Again, using perfect basic strategy.
Craps: A pass line wager, odds on that pass line bet and placing the six or eight.
Baccarat: The bank or player hand.
Slots: Yes, even a cybernetic one-armed bandit can be a good play if it's advertised as a 98 plus percent return machine.

Horace once said: "Gold can be slave or master." So can the wrong casino wager.

15

DEAR MARK: *Every time I chip away (no pun intended) at the casino, they return larger chips than those I'm betting. I get the feeling they want me to cash out and keep what I've just won. Why are they being so polite to a winner?* **Randall C.**

Quite the contrary, Randall. The second you get on a hot streak, casinos prefer pit employees to "change color" or upgrade your chips. No, they're not being courteous, just trying to induce larger play. Because most players don't equate casino chips with real money, it's easy to get caught up in the game and forget what you're actually betting.

Treat all chips, won or lost, like Friday's paycheck—your hard-earned money.

DEAR MARK: *I have a system in roulette where I play all the odd black numbers and if I lose I follow it by playing all the red even numbers. The dealer took note of how I was betting so he knew my style of play. While betting my odd black numbers, I placed $2 on 17 black as the ball was about to drop. Suddenly the dealer reached for my money and handed it back to me. As you probably guessed, it came up 17 black. To say the very least I was extremely upset and demanded to be paid. The dealer said he couldn't pay me because he had already called "no more betting" before I put my bet on 17 black. The pit boss came over and agreed with the dealer's decision. Even though the ball did not land in a slot yet, and the dealer probably knew my style of play, shouldn't I still have been paid?* **Tom D.**

Your question reminds me of the roulette player who sent home this telegram: "System working well—send more money."

As a rule, Tom, the casino wants the dealer to wait to the final "reasonable" moment before he barks "no more bets." The house wants to get as many wagers per decision as possible because they hold a hefty 5.26% advantage over the player on roulette. The long and short of it, Tom, is that every casino has its own set of guidelines it wants its dealers to follow. Additionally, every experienced roulette dealer has his own sense of timing on when to halt wagering.

In this case, Tom, I side with the dealer (casino). The simple solution is to get your bets in early. Better yet, how about finding a new game that does not have such a precipitous house edge? All you need now is a new system.

♠ 9 ♠
Pumping Oxygen into a Casino is NOT a Trick of the Trade

DEAR MARK: *My friend believes that many of the Vegas casinos pump oxygen through the air conditioning system to enrich the air. The purpose is to keep you from sleeping as long and therefore gambling more. I didn't notice any difference in my sleeping habits, but still, my friend insists he's right. Is he?* **Colin I.**

Colin, your friend is full of, of, of, OK, I'll be nice, baloney. What comes to mind every time I hear this rumor are the three Apollo astronauts who died when a small spark combined with oxygen ignited their space capsule creating one of NASA's worst disasters.

According to my neighbor Dick (Captain, South San Francisco Fire Department), "pumping oxygen into a casino would be a tremendous fire hazard that would greatly increase the flammability of all other objects. Any small fire, anywhere in the hotel, would be fanned and magnify itself by pumped oxygen." As for the risk/reward opportunity, no casino would ever entertain the thought.

Of course that doesn't mean the casino doesn't have its share of tricks to part bettors from their cash. Casinos spend tens of thousands of dollars each year studying whether scents, interior design (yes, even that gaudy carpeting) or trying to keep light off the foreheads of customers—which is draining on them from an energy standpoint—will make players stay and play more. If somehow a casino could figure out how to keep each and every patron playing just five more minutes a night, it would add millions to a casino's gross each year.

17

Now back to this ridiculous rumor of pumping oxygen, Colin. It does have a starting point. I believe ground zero comes from Mario Puzo's book, *Fools Die*, where the practice of pumping oxygen was written by Puzo regarding the mythical Las Vegas casino Xanadu. I guess your friend translated this fictional work into reality, but hey, Colin, maybe casinos one day will try decreasing the oxygen to disorient the players even more than they already are.

DEAR MARK: *What is the most popular slot machine in the casino?* **Tara C.**

The bulk of the lucrative slot business has been the exclusive territory of one manufacturer, International Game Technology (IGT). Their bread-and-butter comes from the most popular machine in America: the Red, White and Blue reel slot. And what makes the Red, White and Blue so popular? Player appeal. People flock to the colors that represent America. Players also love the paytable that offers plenty of low and midrange hits with enough high-end hits to keep them coming back for more.

Note here, Tara, that the above description of "hit rewards" comes from IGT company literature, not me. Because most slots typically have a casino advantage well above my recommended two percent, avoid putting those Red, White and Blue machines in your playing arsenal.

DEAR MARK: *In my favorite casino, the Caribbean Stud progressive tote is at $55,200 for a royal flush. How good a wager, and when is it mathematically in my favor?* **Jimbo N.**

Sorry, Jimbo, I can't recommend this wager to anyone. First, note there are 2,598,960 possible poker hands using a standard 52-card deck. Now divide that figure by four (the different suits) and you'll come up with 649,740. Because you don't get to draw any cards in Caribbean Stud, this mathematically is the odds of hitting a royal. Jimbo, one in 649,740 is too big a differential from the $55,200 they plan on paying you for me to endorse this play.

"I hope to break even this week. I need the money."
– VETERAN LAS VEGAS GAMBLER

♠ 10 ♠
Off to the Races

DEAR MARK: *I find horse racing one of the most enjoyable forms of casino gambling. For just $2 I can sit in an air conditioned race book and watch simulcast races from all across America. Wow! Any advice for a newbie horse player?* **Robert A.**

I'm with you, Robert. A splash of stimulation and a $2 wager on a long-shot equine overdue for the glue factory can be an inexpensive diversion from a $25 minimum blackjack game. At $2 that is. But with Nevada's race books offering only pari-mutuel wagering, Robert, the house does hold an 18-22% edge on any straight bet you make at the sports book window.

That said, pony players in the know—not me, I go by the horse's biorhythms—believe the following factors are essential to your chances of picking winners.

1. knowledge of breeding
2. physical specifications of the race track (length, turns, surface, drain -age, etc.)
3. track bias in the horse's previous starts
4. jockey skills
5. trainer skills
6. current form of the horse
7. how the horse likes track conditions
8. horse's ability at today's distance
9. predicted pace of the race
10. how to read a program or a *Daily Racing Form*
11. etc., etc., etc.

It was our beloved first president, George Washington, himself a racehorse owner who once said, "Horse racing is the child of avarice, the brother of iniquity, and the father of mischief."

Gitty up!

DEAR MARK: *I like to plunk down bets on the "Big 6," that carnival type wheel you will find in most casinos. What are the house odds on that game?* **Gary R.**

You do realize, Gary, that you plunk and the dealer snatches. All six wagers on the Big 6 carry a steep house edge. That casino advantage is as follows: 11.1 percent on the $1 spot, 16.6% on the $2, 22.2% on the $5, 18.5% on the $10, 22.2% on the $20, and 24% on either joker.

By betting a steady diet of Big 6 wagers, Gary, you will run out of air speed and altitude quickly.

DEAR MARK: *If, like you say, the house has only a 1.4% advantage on a pass line bet, how can the casino make any money by offering that wager?* **Jordan P.**

It doesn't matter who wins this one bet but who ends up with all the money. The casino realizes few players are sophisticated enough to restrict their craps betting to just smart wagers.

But let's look at the bet in question, Jordan: a pass line wager. If you were to play 100 bets on the pass line, you can expect to win about 49 times and lose the other 51. The casino will gladly take this itty-bitty 49/51 ratio and multiply it by thousands of decisions daily, weekly and yearly, and guarantee themselves a generous long-term profit.

DEAR MARK: *Does the Megabucks machine pay back the same as regular $1 slot machines?* **Mary K.**

Notta chance, Mary. By offering the player a shot at slot immortality, Megabucks shakes you down on the smaller payoffs. It is Megabuck's progressive bonus that allows you to fantasize champagne wishes and caviar dreams. On average, Megabucks returns slightly less than a 90% payback while the typical $1 machine in Nevada averages more than 95%.

DEAR MARK: *When I hear cheering coming from a crap game, does that mean it's a hot game ready for me to dive right in?* **Bruce T.**

Not necessarily, Bruce. The dice might have been sizzling before you come aboard, but that doesn't mean they will stay heated because you're now there. The reason is that your dice timeline—the period you're on the game—is different from the earlier players.

Understand, Bruce, when you join a game in progress, you initiate your own personal sequence of rolls, with the dice possibly going cold from that moment on.

♠ 11 ♠
Pushovers Sit Here

DEAR MARK: *It seems to me that in blackjack the less you know the more right your decisions are. When it comes to splitting pairs, doubling, even hitting certain hands, I take a chance and generally go against common wisdom. Therefore, my thoughts are that it isn't worth the extra trouble to learn the correct strategy.* **Rory B.**

Someone once said. "the first rules of holes is when you are in one, stop digging." Rory, You've got one big shovel.

In blackjack, or any casino game for that matter, the less you know the more you should deride the analysis of anyone who has the knowledge and takes the trouble to study the subject from a mathematical perspective. Depending on how you play blackjack, you can gain the designation of professional player all the way down to a "sucker on a stool."

Using guesswork, your playing style doesn't put you in the professional category; more like a "dupe in action."

DEAR MARK: *Recently on a blackjack game I was ahead by more than $400. The pit boss after a brief introduction comped me a pass to the casino buffet. After eating a so-so meal I came back and proceed to give back all my winnings. In hindsight, isn't the meal offering a way of making me play longer?* **Buddy C.**

Yes, because Nevada Revised Statute176.387 does not allow casinos to use *Crazy Glue* on casino stools to keep players in bondage until they lose all their winnings.

Seriously, Buddy, free buffets are used by casino management primarily to encourage additional gambling. FREE and FOOD are subtle weapons that give the casinos an added firearm in reclaiming what they believe is still their money. The pit boss is simply treating you to a buffet so you feel obligated to play longer. Long enough so that the buffet will cost you $400.

It is much better to learn to win and walk, not stay and suffer (money loss and abdominal duress).

DEAR MARK: *You columns illustrate a biased position when it comes to playing keno. I enjoy gambling while eating and keno is the only game that affords this. I've always liked the fact that for a dollar you could win $25,000. Why are you so anti keno?* **Doris F.**

Because I'm resentful, invidious and jealous. I was one of those kids who never got a box of 64 Crayolas. Always a used eight pack; one broke, one missing. So any game that you mark with a crayon that carries a house percentage higher than the interest you pay on your Visa card, I'm illiberal about.

DEAR MARK: *What does the term "following the shoe" mean in baccarat?* **Phillip H.**

The term simply means whichever side (player or banker) won the last hand, your next bet would be the same. Consequently, if a streak occurs for either side (common in baccarat), you will be riding it for its full duration.

DEAR MARK: *My goal when I play craps is to win $1,000 with a $100 buy-in. Do you feel this is impractical?* **Skip R.**

Bellying up to a crap table with $100 and expecting to win $1,000 is, at best, unrealistic. Personally, I believe it's downright wacky. Odds-on you will lose your C-note long before you win a grand.

Skip, you need to set reasonable win goals, like 50% of your original stake, not 1000% on your money. Far too many players keep upping the ante on what they want to win. This columnist recommends having predetermined loss limits and "realistic" win goals.

It takes internal fortitude to take a small win and run. I'm not asking you to quit while you are on an eventful winning streak, but true winners know how to quit when they are ahead. They don't risk it all to achieve too lofty a reward.

♠ 12 ♠
Finders Keepers, Losers Weepers

DEAR MARK: *You always say check your machine for credits before you leave. Is it true that if I went to play a machine and there were credits left on it by someone I could get in trouble with the casino?* **Beri W.**

Called "sea gulling" in gambling lingo, it is illegal to specifically circle the casino looking for credits on a slot machine. Not even change on the floor. I've seen player impostors given the heave ho (the dreadful permanent 86) for making a full-time occupation of floating the casino looking for easy pickings. Fortunately I have never heard of an unsuspecting patron walking up to a machine with credits, playing them, and being shown the door.

Nevertheless, Beri, before you walk away from any slot machine, don't forget to press the cash-out button. Millions are lost each year by gamblers forgetting their stored credits (winnings).

DEAR MARK: *Though this question is not technically gambling related, I figured you might know the answer. In sweepstakes and contests, do you stand the same chance of winning even if you do not purchase the product (magazines) the company is trying to sell?* **Sally C.**

Sweepstakes, like casinos, by nature tap into the dark heart of the American Dream. Something for nothing! And because sweepstakes entries reach 8 in 10 households, with an estimated 108 million sweepstakes entries received from more than 80 million U.S. households last year, it makes for an excellent question.

Many people believe that if they buy merchandise with their entry they have a better chance of winning a sweepstakes. Not so, states the Direct Marketing Association, the Magazine Publishers of America and the Promotion Marketing Association. All legitimate sweepstakes entries have an equal chance of winning. Federal law requires that no purchase is necessary to win a sweepstakes prize, and legitimate sweepstakes never require any purchase or "deposit" to play or win. This policy is stated on every sweepstakes mailing from law-abiding companies.

23

Also note, Sally, that approximately four out of five sweepstakes entries are sent in without any purchase. Correspondingly, four out of five sweepstakes winners last year came from contestants who didn't purchase a product. But, Sally, I can't state enough that the operative word here is "legitimate." Fraudulent, illegal sweepstakes often require a payment or purchase. These lawless rip-off artists often use names similar to legitimate companies to confuse the consumer. Machiavellian or not, expect to find most sweepstakes entries inferring in large type that you're a "guaranteed winner," small type showing insurmountable odds and computer-generated language that sounds as if you were receiving a personal letter. That, Sally, is the nature of the beast.

Taking into account that your typical sweepstakes odds are a tougher beat than your state lottery, the only way you can avoid both crooked companies and exposing your Visa Platinum to solicited charges is to religiously follow this one cardinal rule. Enter, never purchase.

DEAR MARK: *I don't quite understand what is meant by a pay cycle on a slot machine. Does it mean that over one pay cycle, every possible combination on the reel will appear?* **Melvin V.**

Not quite, Melvin. The term "pay cycle" is a theoretic expression used to describe the number of plays required for the machine to display all the possible winning and non-winning combinations. But, because each and every spin is a random event, a machine won't hit all the possible combinations through any one specific cycle.

DEAR MARK: *I really enjoy your column on the internet, but I have yet to see a discussion on two new table games on the floor: Let it Ride and Caribbean Stud Poker. Obviously, if they have a house advantage above your recommended two percent, I'm not interested. So exactly how high is the house edge on these new games?* **Dan C.**

First, Dan, I must commend you for being the rare breed of gambler who looks at the casino advantage before making a wager.

The house edge for Let it Ride is 3.5% and 5.3% for Caribbean Stud Poker. As for the progressive bonus side bets, the house advantage is 46 an 48 percent respectively.

24

♠ 13 ♠
Please Be the Queen of Spades

DEAR MARK: *Why is it that every time I'm dealt one card short of the royal flush, when I draw I never get the card I need? Just yesterday I was dealt all but the queen of spades, and sure enough, I got the lousy three of hearts. It makes me believe the casino controls who and when someone hits a jackpot. Why can't that queen of spades show up just once?* **Katherine R.**

What do you expect, Katherine? The queen of spades represents Athena, the Greek goddess of war. Pull out a deck of cards and look at her closely. She's the only armed queen in the deck. Even Homer in the *Illiad*, described her as a fierce battle goddess who continually intervened on the side of the Greeks in the Trojan War. Expect her to arbitrate on behalf of the casino every time.

Seriously, Katherine, I could bore you to tears by trying to explain how the pseudo-random number generator determines the cards you will get, but instead, I'll simply describe the difficulties you're up against when fate blesses you with four of the five cards needed for a royal flush.

Because there are 2,598,960 possible poker hands using a 52-card deck, you're going to feel pretty good when your hand is one card shy of gaming ecstasy. But although the big jackpot appears to be only one card away, your chances are really only one in 47 or just over two percent.

Another way to visualize its difficulty is taking a thousand video poker players lucky enough to start with your proposed hand. A ten of spades, jack of spades, king of spades, ace of spades and a three of hearts. Naturally, all in my controlled group will discard the three of hearts, leaving only 21 mathematically hitting the royal flush, then 150 flushes, 128 straights, 191 high pair hands and 510 who think, like you, the big fix is on.

Sorry, Katherine, it's just not as easy as it seems, but keep trying. Someday Athena may look favorably on you.

25

Oh, yes, a final thought. In case you want to know what the remaining better halves of the kings represent? The queen of diamonds is Rachel, wife of Jacob and mother of the twelve sons who founded the twelve tribes of Israel. The queen of clubs is an anagram of Regina, signifying queen. The queen of hearts is Judith of Bavaria, daughter-in-law of Charlemagne. And of course, we've already met Athena.

DEAR MARK: *I would like to know a little about the four suits and their rank from highest to lowest. Does one suit on a video poker machine rank higher than another?* **Joe C.**

Generally no, but occasionally a casino will have a promotion with designated video poker machines paying higher jackpots if certain straights, flushes or royals are in a particular suit. There are also a few video poker machines that pay a mega-jackpot if you hit a royal flush in a predetermined suit with cards in sequential order. (Example: 10 of Hearts, JH, QH, KH and Ace of Hearts.) And what are the possibilities of hitting a consecutive card royal in a prearranged suit? Let's just say, Joe, it's easier to hit your New York state lottery.

Now for some bar stool trivia. Though cards have existed since the earliest Asian civilizations, France had the greatest influence on the creation of the modern deck. They eliminated the major arcana and combined the knight and page, reduced the size of the deck to 52 cards and simplified the suit symbols to red diamonds and hearts, black spades and trefoils (clover leaves). They were produced in mass quantity after Johann Gutenberg invented the printing press in 1455, and the four suits reflect the structure of the medieval society. Hearts—priesthood; spades—nobility; clubs—peasantry; diamonds—the wealthy merchant class.

By the way, after Gutenberg printed the 1,284-page Gutenberg Bible on the printing press, the second impressions made were of playing cards.

"SUCKERS HAVE NO BUSINESS WITH MONEY ANYWAY."
– CANADA BILL JONES, LEGENDARY THREE-CARD MONTE DEALER

♠ 14 ♠
Split Decision

DEAR MARK: *We are deciding to make a family trip to either Las Vegas or Disneyland. We have three children all under the age of eight. I would like to know your recommendations and experiences (good/bad).* **Elise G.**

Elise, if you're looking for total family entertainment, choose the latter and take your family to Disneyland. Don't get me wrong, I LOVE Las Vegas—just not as a family destination. Because it's only fair you get a second opinion, let me bring in my expert on such matters—the biggest Las Vegas promoter I know. No, not Steve Wynn, my 10-year-old son, Nick.

Mark: All right, Nick, tell my readers your choice of a vacation, Disneyland or Las Vegas?

Nick: Las Vegas! It's rad.

Mark: Come on, it's not for kids. We were there on a Tuesday during a school break and I could count all the families I saw on one hand. (Note: Before you write in and call me a numskull stating it's during the school year, so don't expect kids, we were at Disneyland the following two days and it was swarming with families.)

Nick: That just means we have the whole place to ourselves.

Mark: Okay, name some of the things you thought were "rad."

Nick: The Luxor arcade. The coolest I've ever seen.

Mark: In two hours, you spent more in quarters than a Disneyland Passport costs for the day.

Nick: We both liked that pirate stuff at the Treasure Island Casino.

Mark: The pyrotechnics and the pirate ship battle were good, but don't forget we waited for one hour so we could view it from the front, and you complained you were being squished to death. Plus it lasted only five minutes.

Nick: I've got something, big fella. I can't wait to go on that roller-coaster on that tall building.

Mark: I'm drawing the line here, Nick. No way am I going to allow you to get on a roller coaster that's 1,149 feet in the air. Wait till you're 18, better yet, 21. Case closed.

Nick: Chicken!

Mark: And one further thing about the Stratosphere tower roller coaster....

Nick: Bawk, bawk, bawk, bawk, bawk.... Anyway, I thought the amusement park at the MGM was way cool.

Mark: We were there off season, not during the summer, when the temperatures rise to over 110 degrees, long lines and you're limited to just 12 rides. Overpriced, no matter what they charge. (Currently, you must be over 48 inches tall to go on any of the rides.)

Nick: You have to admit, Dad, the MGM building is awesome. All the buildings are.

Mark: You mean I've got a future architect in the family? NOT! You just wanted a $20 souvenir from each location.

Nick: Well, they at least offer you something to do once you're inside.

Mark: Whether it's the boat ride on the Nile at the Luxor or viewing the Emerald Forest in the MGM, cha-ching, cha-ching, it cost bucks, very little is free. And all the walking to and from, I've got blisters....

Nick: Your whining!

Mark: True, but I don't know what's worse. Blisters from all the concrete afoot, or our taxi bill for two days: $148.

Nick: Well, I know something the big guy really liked—the buffets.

Mark: Guilty as charged.

Nick: And when I went on stage during Lance Burton's Magic Show, not once, but twice!

Mark: Nick, you couldn't find a prouder father. Of course, not everyone scores front row, center seats and has a son with the best "pick me" handwave in his fourth grade class. Let's take a break, Nick.

Elise, the "Sin City" element of Las Vegas is still alive and well, so don't expect Vegas to be the "Orlando of the West." Example: I took a solitary walk between the Flamingo Hilton and the Luxor, estimation one mile, and 47 times I was approached and handed four color brochures of fantasy girls, willing and able, to make my visit to Las Vegas worth—use your imagination. Retreating with my wife and Nick in tow, discretion worked to a point, with only nine handbill distributors pushing their wares on me. I guess on the plus side, 38 respected the institution of the family, but the visual effects remain. Those circulars are scattered all over the sidewalk.

Nick: I'm back. Any other questions, Dad?

Mark: Sure, one more, Nick. Your final word on Las Vegas.

Nick: When can we go again?

Mark: My final thought, Elise. Baby strollers and high rollers don't mix.

A final thought. The total expenditure for two days in Las Vegas was $739. Disneyland, $466. The following is directed to the gaming industry. Guess how much I gambled (total) when our family went to Las Vegas? $20. And when Nick doesn't go? Let's just say, MORE! Your "family theme" idea is way off the mark.

♠ 15 ♠
You Lose, Just Less Often

DEAR MARK: *Every basic strategy card, blackjack book, and yes, you, recommend splitting eights against a dealer 10. Well, fear gets the better of me, and I depart from correct play and just hit instead of splitting the pair. So what should I do about a hand that always seems to haunt me? Hit, split or play the hunch?* **Scott N.**

You're right, Scott, eights against a 10 is a phantasmal hand that stalks most players like Marley's ghost.

As my readers know, blackjack is a game where the proper hit, stand, splitting and doubling decisions are necessary in order to cut the house edge down to a minimum. These proper decisions are called basic strategy and have been arrived at by computer simulations of millions of hands.

But fallacious logic tells you that splitting this hand creates two losers. Seems every time you split those eights you get, at best, two 10s. Then the dealer always has a nine or 10 in the hole, and bang, the jingling you hear is not Marley's forged chains but all your money falling into the dealer's tray.

So what happens to the average player? He starts deviating from basic strategy because FEAR sets in. The FEAR is actually **F**alse **E**vidence **A**ppearing **R**eal. FEAR camouflages the logic of computer studies. But according to basic strategy, the proper move is to split 8s if the game you're playing doesn't allow surrender. Why? Because you will lose more money in the long run if you hit instead of splitting. Mathematically, when you just hit the hand, you will lose $51 for every $100 wagered. However, if you split, you will lose $44 for every $100 bet. A seven dollar difference for every hundred dollars wagered.

Granted, Scott, it's a character builder to come out of pocket with additional money, but the key behind basic strategy is: Win more money not necessarily more hands.

29

DEAR MARK: *I've been around computers since 1978 and some folks even call me a computer genius. My new project is to develop a hand-held computer I can conceal in my pocket and try counting cards with much more accuracy. What are the risks/consequences if caught with a hand-held computing device in my possession in a casino?* **Anonymous**

Dear Anonymous, allow me to let Beavis and Butthead spell it out for you: "Just because you own a computer doesn't mean you still can't be stupid."

DEAR MARK: *I have been following your advice and making casino bets that have less than a two percent house advantage. I now consider myself a reformed player. My blockhead brother on the other hand makes bets with no rhyme or reason. Since we both play craps, show me why my pass line bet versus his favorite bet, hardway sixes and eights, will always do better?* **Susan M.**

Susan, by using a simple mathematical formula, I will prove that by playing smart, your play will generally outperform your brother's.

Let's first analyze your action, Susan. A pass line bet, with no odds, has a house advantage of 1.4%. With a $5 wager and 50 playing decisions per hour, your theoretical loss (all bets lose over time) is $5 X 50 X 0.014, or $3.50 per hour. Relatively cheap entertainment. In comparison, your brother's bet, the hard six or eight, has a house advantage of 9.1%. The damage to his bankroll would be $5 X 50 X 0.091, or $22.75 in the same amount of time. Multiply that by 15 hours of play and you've got a sniveling, unhappy camper with a long car ride home.

Sibling rivalry aside, glad to see you're reforming your play. Now let's convert the blockhead.

A father and his five-year-old son came home after an afternoon trip. "How did you enjoy the zoo, Johnny?" asked his mother. "Oh, it was great," Johnny replied. "And Daddy really enjoyed it. Especially when one of the animals came racing home at 25 to 1."

♠ 16 ♠
Strike When They Ask

DEAR MARK: *When a pit boss approaches and introduces himself, then asks if there is anything I need, is that an appropriate time to ask for a comp?* **Danielle M.**

Absolutely. Anytime pit bosses or casino hosts offer you anything, they're not going out of their way to be overly friendly, but your level of action probably warrants some casino perks. Meaning, your cash play deserves a comp, and since they're asking, you should start taking.

Your reply, Danielle, from this moment forward, should be immediate and direct. "As a matter of fact, there is," you should reply. "What are the chances of you comping me a dinner?" Why do you have to be forceful? Because even though most floor personnel have some form of comping authority, you generally have to initiate the request.

There are times that you'll find your front-line pit boss can't board you for the night or allow you to go on a champagne and escargot feeding frenzy in their gourmet restaurant, but a buffet or a show room pass is within their limits. If they balk, the standard "Maybe I should take my patronage next door" always seems to work.

Strike when they ask, Danielle, because if your bankroll or bet size spirals downward, the casino's gratuity will probably wane accordingly.

DEAR MARK: *I got in a beef with casino management in New Jersey over how rudely I was treated on a blackjack game. Not only did I decided not to play at this casino anymore, but I stopped payment on a $20 check that I had written there. Well, I think it has come back to haunt me because recently when I tried to cash a personal check in Las Vegas, the cashier refused. What's the big deal? It was only $20.* **Anonymous**

The "big deal," at least in the casino industry's eyes, is that you stiffed them. And the penalty for your ingenuous act? Blackballing you from cashing checks in most casinos nationwide. When you tried to cash that check in Las Vegas, the cashier most likely ran you through Central Credit—the TRW of the gaming industry. Bingo, you came up hot. A little disagreement and $20 later, you're an undesirable—according to a computer of course.

Solution—that is if you want to cash checks in a casino again—is to pay off the check, include a graceful apology, then, with knee pads on, appeal to the cage manager to get your indiscretion taken off Central Credit's computers. Still peeved and won't give in? You could always cash checks for $10 or less. Though casinos are required to comply with federal laws on credit approvals, some get around that by issuing credit for $10 or less without a Central Credit check.

No, it's not the appropriate way to handle your predicament, but then, I believe in betting only what you can afford to lose and avoid check cashing, and casino credit, altogether.

DEAR MARK: *Why is it that when so many dealers get halfway through the deck, they shuffle up? It really slows down the game.* **David V.**

Because management has egg-shell nerves when it comes to players using their brains—card counters.

This fallacious behavior is unjustified and to casino executives whose belief is that their quarterly reports are in jeopardy by cerebral thinkers I offer a personal challenge: Conduct time and motion studies of your blackjack games. What the stewards of gambling will find out is that blackjack becomes more profitable for the casino when the dealer's shuffle points are deeper. By allowing additional deck penetration, the dealers will pitch more hands per hour and the action will more than make up for an occasional loss by a card sharpie. Besides, they employ pit bulls to run off the counters anyway.

"Don't gamble the rent money or you'll land up sleeping on the park bench." – CAPT. SUMMER FUN, RET.

♠ 17 ♠
Right Place, Wrong Timing

DEAR MARK: *Recently I got my first royal flush. That was the good news. The bad news is I only had two coins in it when it hit. Would I have still gotten a royal flush had I inserted the maximum amount of coins?* **Jennifer G.**

No, but not for the reason you're probably thinking. Many, many players believe that video poker machines are programmed to avoid a royal flush because the maximum amount of coins was inserted. As stated many times in this column, machines do not operate with artificial intelligence programmed to hit royals when you have less than the maximum amount of coins in the machine.

The reason you would have received a different hand, Jennifer, is because in the short amount of time it would have taken to insert the additional coins you didn't play, the machine's random number generator (RNG) would have cycled to another outcome. A video poker machines RNG will typically continue to crunch those 1s and 0s until you hit the deal button. As many as a million hands per minute. So unless you pushed the deal button at the correct millisecond, Jennifer, no, the proverbial royal flush with five coins inserted would not have appeared.

DEAR MARK: *If black appeared six times in a row on a roulette table, which way should I wager on the seventh spin, black or red?* **Jim D.**

Many self-proclaimed experts believe they can find trends in roulette by watching the wheel. For that reason, over the years I've facetiously asked them the following question: Black has appeared on a non-biased roulette wheel 30 straight times. Which way should you place your next bet? Would you a) bet black because of the established streak, B) bet red because it's way overdue or C) not wager.

33

Well, Jim, the first two answers are right as well as wrong. No amount of past history on a random non-biased wheel guarantees the outcome of the next spin. Each spin is an independent event, and the law of averages does not apply to any one desultory spin.

But Deal Me In readers know the answer I'm looking for is C. They know that over the long run their losses will be 5.26%. This casino edge is a tad bit too high for the readership of this column.

DEAR MARK: *What are your thoughts about the blackjack game where you see the dealer's hole card in advance?* **Vince R.**

Stick with the old tried and true, Vince. This form of blackjack is not worth playing. Because you lose pushes and only receive even money on blackjacks, the house edge is 2% higher than normal blackjack.

DEAR MARK: *Which is a better wager on a crap game? An "any craps" bet or a "craps-eleven" bet?* **Gary A.**

NEITHER, with one exception. Your dial-a-psychic is accurate 100% of the time.

An "any craps" bet is wagering that 2, 3, or 12 will be the result of the next roll. With a payoff of 7 to 1, the house edge is 11.1%. A "craps-eleven," or "horn" bet as it's typically called, is a bet on the next roll that the 2, 3, 11, or 12 will appear. If any other number rolls, you lose. Though the payoff varies from casino to casino, the house edge on a horn bet is always more than 12%. A piratical house advantage if ever there was one.

*"Whoever said gambling started in Nevada is nuts.
Try Wall Street!"* – ROGER RIGHT

♠ 18 ♠
Slots at 35,000 Feet?

DEAR MARK: *Any truth to the rumor that I will be able to gamble on a flight from Cleveland to Las Vegas?* **Laurie H.**

You mean wager that your flight will arrive on time? Take the six-to-five against.

No, Laurie, you won't see the captain turning off the no-betting signs in preparation for your landing. Though some airlines have gambling systems tested and ready to go, don't expect to lose more than your luggage on your next flight. A friendly wager in the sky only applies to international flights—not flights that take off or land in the United States. The 1994 Gorton Amendment bans gambling on flights by an international carrier that begins or ends in this country.

Laurie, I just cannot foresee even lobbied politicians of unsound mind allowing holiday travelers to arrive at their vacation destination pauperized.

DEAR MARK: *Twice in past columns you have stated unequivocally that casinos do not cheat customers. You also mentioned the possibility of a rogue dealer affecting my chances of winning. Could you please give me an example of something a dishonest dealer could do to change the odds in the casino's favor?* **Billy T.**

An example would be of an unscrupulous dealer who *preferential shuffles*. Here a dealer is counting the deck down (card counting) and is aware of all the cards that have been dealt. If a lot of high cards have been previously pitched, meaning the deck is now rich in small cards, creating an apparent disadvantage for the player, the rogue dealer keeps dealing. On the other hand, if many small cards have surfaced, allowing a positive expectation for the player, the dealer would shuffle.

By card counting, the unethical dealer now has total control over any favorable situation the player might have had.

DEAR MARK: *Nothing irks me more than when two pit bosses in the same casino interpret the rules differently. I had a pit boss allow me to replay my hand (I didn't signal a hit and the dealer hit me anyway for a bust). Another pit boss instructed the dealer to take my wife's money on an identical error one hour later. Don't they play from the same rule book?* **David M.**

Floormen, a.k.a. dealing referees, at times render contrary decisions. Calling a particular play differently ultimately confuses casino clientele. You, and yes, even the dealer, have a very legitimate gripe against management on inconsistent calls.

Casinos where customer service prevails always side with the player unless the mistake is illegal or egregious. Why lose a customer for life over a $10 error? They realize the math is always on the side of the casino.

Funny how it works, David. When the house lets you keep your mistake, they always seem to get it back on the next hand.

DEAR MARK: *There is a company in Europe selling devices that electronically jackpot slot machines. Is this legal in Nevada? What is the penalty for using it?* **Robert L.**

Why waste your money, Robert? Try this instead. Hoist a sledgehammer in the air, angle it at 45 degrees, then bring it crashing down on the polished glass face of the paytable. That should trigger the hopper to release the coins. Either way, the penalty is the same. A ward of the state, AKA, PRISON! Good behavior should get you out in five.

DEAR MARK: *Is there a specific time when a gambler should get up and walk away from a table when winning?* **Wayne D.**

The two hardest times to leave a casino are when you're ahead or when you're behind. That, Wayne, is why all gamblers should set loss limits and win goals.

Though your question lacked precise information, like how much you bet, how long, which games, where, etc., setting specific win goals such as doubling your money, AND STICKING TO THEM, is the correct money management strategy when it comes to bidding your farewells.

♠ 19 ♠
The Odds are 3 to 1 Against You Beating the Casino

DEAR MARK: *Why has the term "odds" been so closely associated with gambling?* **Terry K.**

The laws of probability, Terry, on which odds are based, are as highly respected a branch of mathematics as geometry, trigonometry or differential calculus. Odds are used in business, science, military planning, mortality rates and virtually all human endeavors—including gambling.

Most gamblers don't realize it, but every time they enter a casino the odds are 3 to 1 against them no matter which game they play. First, you battle the casino percentages on each and every game; second, you combat the casino's tactics that make you lose; and third, you fight the demons from within.

There is your 3 to 1 against.

DEAR MARK: *In blackjack, why is it that when the deck is rich in aces and face cards it favors the player?* **Gary C.**

There are two reasons. First, blackjacks will appear more often when there is a higher proportion of aces in the deck, and as you know blackjacks pay the player 3 to 2. Second, the dealer will bust more when he has a "stiff" (12 through 16). The player, given the same opportunity, would stand on stiffs, whereas the dealer is forced by the rules of the game to hit away and hopefully bust.

DEAR MARK: *My friend believes that all roulette tables operate on streaks and you should only wager on numbers that have recently appeared. I believe, and I am sure you will concur, that he is full of it. I could use some help convincing my friend.* **Steve B.**

37

A streak is nothing more than a backward glimpse at probability and should not be taken into consideration in most, if not all, gaming situations.

Roulette wheels, Steve, do not operate with artificial intelligence nor do they have any way of remembering which past numbers have hit. Each spin is an independent event that is not controlled by past spins.

Your friend's theory has zero merit.

DEAR MARK: *Could you please explain how much the progressive meter rises on both your average slot and video poker machine?* **Jane B.**

The rate at which the meter progresses upward is based on a pre-set percentage of all the money cycled through the machine. The meter rates will vary from machine to machine, casino to casino. If you are playing an individual progressive, expect an advance rate of five to 10 percent of the money played. Example: A dollar wagered, the jackpot goes up 10¢. Machines that are tied together, like a bank (carousel) or networked slots like Megabucks or Quartermania, involve a much lower progressive rate. In return, you are provided a mega jackpot—a.k.a. big, big bucks.

On your typical video poker machine, the meters rise on the average of between .25 and two percent with one percent being the industry average.

DEAR MARK: *If I may, a quick history question. Who invented the slot machine?* **Ted G.**

The first mechanical slot machine, the Liberty Bell, was invented in 1895 by Charles Fey, a San Francisco mechanic. Fey's machine housed three spinning reels, each decorated with diamonds, spades, hearts and one cracked Liberty Bell per reel. When the bells lined up, they produced your biggest payoff: 10 nickels.

If you are ever in Reno, Ted, the original Liberty Bell is on display at the Liberty Belle Saloon & Restaurant, on 4250 S. Virginia.

DEAR MARK: *The video poker card that comes with your Hooked on Winning audio cassette series states that a 2-card royal (Ace, no 10) is a more powerful hand than a 2-card royal (10, no Ace). Why is that?* **Barney G.**

A two card royal with an ace (jack of hearts, ace of hearts) is a preferable hand because if you draw an additional ace, you will get your initial wager returned for the pair of aces. Whereas if you were to draw a second 10, zilch is your payoff.

♠ 20 ♠
The Correct Spelling is ALBUQUERQUE

DEAR MARK: *This is not exactly a casino gambling question but an inquiry regarding bar betting strategies. Why is it that I am always buying free drinks? It does not matter if it's trivia or a magic trick, I am always duped into paying. Help!* **James S.**

Every tavern I have patronized has at least five bar-stool regulars who can spell Albuquerque. In the real world no one can spell it.

You won't be a patsy for free drinks if you heed this classic warning from Damon Runyon: "Son, no matter how far you travel, or how smart you get, always remember this: someday, somewhere, a guy is going to come up to you and show you a nice brand-new deck of cards on which the seal has not been broken, and this guy is going to offer to bet you that the jack of spades will jump out of this deck and squirt cider in your ear. But, son, do not bet him, for as sure as you do, you are going to get an ear full of cider."

DEAR MARK: *Are not the rules better for roulette in Atlantic City than in Las Vegas?* **Jay G.**

Only on one wager, Jay. When you make an even-money bet (red/black, odd/even, 1-18/9-36) in Atlantic City, you lose only half your wager if the roulette ball lands on 0 or 00. These outside wagers cut the house edge down from 5.26 to 2.63%.

Keep in mind, Jay, that this advantage is only in effect for even-money bets. For even better value, Las Vegas offers single zero roulette tables at numerous casinos. A single zero game will give the casino only a 2.7% edge on all roulette bets.

DEAR MARK: *I have only been to the casinos three times but have come home a winner on each occasion. I operate strictly by a "feel" for certain machines. Ever hear of consistent winners that base their skill on "feelings"?* **Dusty R.**

I am willing to wager dollars to donuts that I can prove with 100% certainty that you do not possess such an ability. I bet you want me to prove it. Well, Bob, if you answer my question, "Yes, I go to work every Monday morning," then you don't have such skills.

DEAR MARK: *Thank you for the advice on playing the single-zero roulette game at the Monte Carlo. My wife broke even and I actually won $200. I do have a question regarding the single zero game. Is the game I played at the Monte Carlo in Las Vegas an exact duplicate in rules as a roulette table at the real Monte Carlo in Europe?* **Paul L.**

Not quite, Paul. A true European single-zero wheel offers a rule called "en prison." If you make an even money bet and the ball lands on zero, the croupier doesn't rake in your wager. Instead, your bet is "imprisoned" or held hostage, and you are forced to let it ride until the next spin. If your bet wins, you can remove it from the table.

What is exciting about this wager is that it cuts the house edge on even money bets in half, down to a very respectable 1.35%. This makes it one of the better bets in European casinos.

DEAR MARK: *Is there ever a time when you would double down for less in blackjack?* **Sal G.**

Never is the correct answer. Because you only double down when you are more likely to win the hand than lose, you always want to wager the maximum amount. It is the double downs and blackjacks that take your blackjack play from the red to the black. Don't shortchange yourself in these situations.

"Poker is one of the most fascinating gambling games, because it combines three elements: skill, luck and psychology. It is this combination which draws millions of players to card tables around America." – J. EDWARD ALLEN

♠ 21 ♠
How Gambling and Arby's
are Historically Related

DEAR MARK: *My friend and I are long-time day trippers to Atlantic City. We have a couple of sandwiches riding on the outcome of this wager. As you can tell we're not big bettors. Our question is; who was the first player to make a wager in Atlantic City? I believe it was Frank Sinatra, whereas my friend thinks it was another member of the Rat Pack, Dean Martin. Who's right?* **Marvin K.**

Neither of you wins the light repast. It was a $10 pass line bet by Steve Lawrence that made Atlantic City gambling history on Memorial Day, 1978.

Incidentally, did you know that the invention of sandwich is directly related to gambling? No kidding! The next time you're enjoying a double cheddar, large fry and an Oreo cookie shake, thank the Earl of Sandwich (1718-1792). He loved to gamble so much he had his cortege bring him meats, bread and cheese so he wouldn't have to abandon the gambling parlors. Hence, the sandwich.

DEAR MARK: *Is blackjack still the number one game in Las Vegas? It seems I'm seeing fewer and fewer 21 tables and more and more slots.* **Grant G.**

If I could be "Gambling Czar" for just one day, collecting casino profits on just one game, it would not be the casino win at blackjack but of the 25¢ slot machine. Yes, the quarter machine takes in more in net profit for the casino ($2.6 billion in Nevada) than blackjack, baccarat, craps, roulette, keno and the sports books combined.

Yes, Grant, you are astute in you observations. Vegas is becoming an adult pinball palace.

DEAR MARK: *When you have a 16 in blackjack, would you advise surrendering against a face card? Also could you please explain the difference between early and late surrender?* **Sara G.**

Surrender is an option in which the casinos allow players to "surrender" half their original bet total after they have examined their first two cards and have viewed the dealer up card.

If the casino's blackjack rules permit surrender, jump on their offer. Let's face it, Sara, a 16 is a garbage hand faced off against a 10. The best move when dealt dealer debris is to relinquish half your bet. Never, Sara, think of surrender as giving up half your wager, just getting back half your probable loss.

Early surrender permits a player to relinquish half her wager even if the dealer has a blackjack. With late surrender, if the dealer possesses a blackjack, the player loses her complete bet.

DEAR MARK: *With all the different types of video poker machines to select from, how's a customer to choose which machine to play?* **Gerry B.**

There are more than a hundred different video poker machines to choose from. Games like Joker Poker, Louisiana Jacks, Gator Poker, etc., offer you a supermarket selection, but all have different paytables needing distinct playing strategies.

I recommend learning and limiting your play to two, like my favorites, Deuces Wild and Jacks-or-Better.

DEAR MARK: *What are your thoughts regarding those shuffling machines found on blackjack games?* **Carrie C.**

No aficionado of shuffling machines here, in spite of these shuffle mechanisms finding wide acceptance by casino operators and players alike. With a Shufflemaster, a leading industry shuffle machine, dealers do not have to waste time manually shuffling cards. From the casino perspective, time is money. The more hands per hour the better. From a player's perspective speed kills in a casino environment. The more time you are exposed to the house advantage, the more it will wreak havoc on your bankroll.

I recommend finding a table with the fewest decks possible. This forces the dealer to constantly shuffle and not expose you to any casino edge while shuffling.

♠ 22 ♠
Inside a Cybernetic
One-Armed Bandit

DEAR MARK: *On the weekends, do casinos make adjustments on their video poker machines to make more money?* **Sam K.**

Do you mean do casinos take a screwdriver to their slots on the weekends to tighten them up? No way. It is not cost effective for the casino to continually alter the payouts on their machines. To alter the percentage return in their favor on a video game, the casino must, by law, make a hardware change. You do this by swapping out an internal component, the ROM portion of the microprocessor chip. ROM, or read only memory, is a chip the slot manufacturer provides the casino. This is the chip that tells the video poker machine to pay 9 coins for a full house, 6 coins for a flush. Additionally, they would have to physically change the glass payout schedule on their machines.

What you could see is a seasonal wholesale change to improve their theoretical hold by making all 9/6 machines to 8/5 bandits. By changing to all 8/5 machines, the house holds an additional 3% edge on each and every machine.

DEAR MARK: *Is there a way that the casino can program a video poker machine so that a royal flush never appears?* **Shanon B.**

Can, yes. Would? Never!

What you have described is called secondary decision programming. A good programmer could write code that allows the computer within to stop a hand that is about to be dealt in favor of a different hand. This would prevent big winning hands like royal flushes from appearing their theoretical number of times.

In a highly regulated industry like casinos, it is safe to assume honesty in programming.

43

DEAR MARK: *When I am dealt the first five cards on a video poker machine, are the draw cards already sitting behind the cards I want to discard, or are they dealt from the top of the deck?* **Ed. P.**

It depends, Ed, on the company who produced the slot or how old the machine is. In the past, the majority of video poker machines operated using parallel dealing. This is where all 10 cards are dealt simultaneously, meaning, you are dealt both the display cards and their draw replacements. Discard that dreadful four of clubs and the seven of diamonds, which you didn't need, was sitting behind it all along. Today, the new machines employ serial dealing. Here replacement cards are dealt right from the top of the deck—similar to a live poker game.

Because the cards are shuffled and displayed randomly, neither way has any effect on the outcome.

DEAR MARK: *What are the chances of hitting the lottery twice in one lifetime. Has it ever happened?* **Milton G.**

In a perfect world we all would win the lottery once, shoot scratch golf and drive a Mercedes. But that wasn't perfect enough for divorced convenience-store manager Evelyn Marie Adams of New Jersey when she won her state's lottery twice within a four-month span in 1985. The odds against Ms. Adams winning the double bonanza were 15 trillion to one. Fifteen trillion, Milton, is three thousand times the number of people on this planet.

Since then, seven others have joined the elite fraternity of repeat lottery winners.

DEAR MARK: *How much edge does the casino have in blackjack?* **Jay B.**

It strictly depends on the skill level of each individual player. Against the average Joe the casino has about a two percent edge. A hunch or superstitious player can easily give back eight percent.

Depending on the rules of a particular casino, a Deal Me In reader who uses perfect basic strategy has only a half of a percent disadvantage. They also get rated and work the casino over for comps. Because many casinos give back between 20 to 40 percent of the expected win—not the actual win—in player gratuities, the *Deal Me In* player actually shows a positive expectation when playing blackjack.

♠ 23 ♠
Bankrupt in Three Minutes

DEAR MARK: *Since I don't gamble very often and chances of losing eight in a row are very remote, don't you think it's logical to double my wager every time I lose?* **Albert M.**

I see your logic, if you call it logic, but it isn't. What you are describing is called the Martingale System, a historic name for doubling up after every loss. In essence, you the gambler double your previous bet (after a loss) to recoup that loss plus win back your initial wager. It is probably—no, IT IS—the worst money management system you can use. You would think, logically, this form of betting is foolproof because you have to win sooner or later.

The problem is, you don't have an inexhaustible bankroll, and our friends who own the casinos will limit the maximum size of your wager. Also, ask any gambler you know if six or eight losses in a row is not unusual. I'm experiencing it now with a computer program that picks the pros in football.

But Albert, I really want you to think this through. Here's you. You bet $2 and lose, then $4 to recoup your losses. Then $8, $16, $32, $64, $128, $256, $512. Ka-ching, Kaa-ching, you invested $1,020 just to get your measly two bucks back. Oops, but you were playing on a game that had a table limit of $200. A string of six defeats and the casino automatically protects itself plus sets your loss limit at $252. Wiped out, Albert, in less than three minutes.

The Martingale system is not logical, it's downright lethal. It's so obvious, Albert. No more, please.

DEAR MARK: *What is a hardway number on a crap game and is it a good bet?* **Steve. R.**

A hardway wager is a 4-6-8-10, but only paired up as a 2-2, 3-3, 4-4, 5-5 combination. For example; if you have a hard six wager, a pair of 3-3s would have to roll for you to win. Not a 2-4 or 5-1 dice roll. Is it a good bet? No! House advantage on a hardway 6 or 8 is 9.1 percent. A hardway 4 or 10 has an 11.1 percent casino edge. Readers of *Deal Me In* only make wagers that have a house advantage of two percent or less.

Steve, say adios to this wager.

DEAR MARK: *On my last two trips to Las Vegas I have found slots ($1 machines at the Stratosphere) advertising a return of 98%. I didn't seem to get a decent return on them. Shouldn't the casino, in such a regulated business like gambling, at least pay back the percentage they advertise?* **Dottie C.**

When a casino advertises that its slot machines return 98 percent, it means the machine is pre-programmed "over the long run" to return 98¢ of every dollar played. Don't come to expect that for each dollar inserted you will automatically get 98¢ dribbling back into the tray. The operative phrase here is "over the long run." A "long run" could mean weeks, months, and even years on any given machine.

But let's assume the machine you were playing was paying off 98¢ for each and every dollar bet. Using a liberal definition of the word "good" machine, we'll allow the casino a measly 2% edge. Well, Dottie, if you were to insert $60 per minute into a 98% payback slot machine (not difficult on a dollar machine at $3 a whack using a credit button), you will lose about $72 an hour. Multiply that by eight hours of play and you will come up $576 short in the purse. Even on those advertised high payback machines, the casino still has a way of grinding away at your gambling capital.

The way you avoid this $576 grind is to behave more conservatively by playing on smaller denomination machines (25¢), for shorter increments of time. Casino operators know all to well that such cautious behavior has negative implications on the casino win for the house. They would much prefer you ante-up silver slugs and play all day.

Oh, by the way, Dottie, all too often players like you believe that the casino is in the gambling business. Wrong! They are in the math business. On pre-programmed slot machines that give the house a certain percentage return, you are the only one doing the gambling here.

"Blackjack is the only casino game an amateur can learn to play and at which he can definitely win." – LAWRENCE REVERE

♠ 24 ♠
Extrasensory Behavior on a Crap Game Doesn't Work

DEAR MARK: *When I shoot craps, I have the feeling that a hot roll will always be stopped by a change in the dealers, someone touching the dice, someone crowding the shooter or the dealer giving out the two dice on a seven, eleven or craps. Is this my imagination or is there any kind of truth to it?* **Doug C.**

With all due respect, Doug, your false-premise gambling beliefs are based on an illogical point of view. All too many players use the dial-a-psychic approach on the next toss of the dice when something whimsical happens on the game. I believe the true answer lies in the definition of the word superstition.

Superstition: groundless belief in a supernatural agencies; a popular belief held without reason.

DEAR MARK: *I was wondering, isn't it better to play on a loose jacks or better 6/5 video poker machine than on a very tight full-pay jacks or better 9/6 video poker machine?* **Stanton T.**

No such animal exists in the green felt jungle. Because every hand is dealt randomly, tightness and looseness of a video poker machine are strictly based on the machine's paytable. A 6/5 paytable (6 coins returned for a full house, 5 for a flush with one coin inserted) would be considered tight, no, very tight; whereas a 9/6 machine (9 for a full house, 6 for a flush) would be loose.

47

DEAR MARK: *What is the dumbest thing you ever did in a casino?* **Jim C.**

Facetiously, working in one for 18 years. I burned out so many times they started calling me "Refried Pilarski."

More seriously, my early dabblings in gambling where those of your typical player— playing all the wrong games, the wrong wagers on those games, the wrong way. Ten spot Keno, 15 team sports parlay cards, field bets on a crap game, the Big 6; that was me, making grade school wagers on a limited pay grade (my salary).

DEAR MARK: *What are the chances of any one number showing up four times in a row on a roulette table?* **Anita G.**

On a double-zero game, once every 2,085,136 spins. As a matter of fact, Anita, I saw it happen once, not with one croupier, but with three separate dealers. I was a pit boss at Bill's Lake Tahoe Casino when dealer A spun the number 25. After making his payoffs he went on his break and dealer B stepped in to spin 25 twice consecutively. She was relieved to go home for the evening, then dealer C immediately twirled 25 again.

A sleuth roulette player would have immediately jumped on this game, figuring it was a biased wheel in need of repair. In this instance it was hardly worth mortgaging the house. Single-zero never appeared again over the next seven hours of my shift, nor were any of the numbers in its wheel section coming up with abnormal frequency.

DEAR MARK: *Why is it that when a slot mechanic opens a slot machine the machine stops paying? Is there any hanky panky going on?* **Tim C.**

No need to worry, Tim. A slot machine is usually opened to fill the hopper with more coins or to check for an internal malfunction. The random number generator continues to work even when the slot attendant opens the door. This should not affect the casino keeping "up to" 20¢ of every dollar you put in.

If you feel uncomfortable playing a previously opened machine, you can always move your hind end to another stool.

♠ 25 ♠
Getting Bent Out of Shape

DEAR MARK: *I was listening to a radio talk show about casino gambling when a caller claimed he does well in blackjack by looking for warps. Well, the guest on the show didn't give a response because the host went to a commercial and they didn't come back to the subject. So, Mark, what is a warp?* **Rhonda A.**

In the casino industry, we call it a "dealer tell," meaning, a dealer who gives away information that the casino believes players shouldn't possess. In this case, when a dealer checks the hole card under tens or aces, some inexperienced dealers will unknowingly bend those cards upwards. This will cause the tens and aces to have a different shape than the rest of the cards in the deck. With this information, the sharp-eyed player believes he knows the dealer's hole card by its disfigured state—which is known as "playing the warps."

But believe me, Rhonda, pit bosses who aren't asleep standing up are always on the lookout for dealers who hack their cards to death, and they'll correct this transgression. How effective is this type of play? Well, if you knew the hole card, it could be very lucrative, but it still comes down to casino management's ability to monitor their pit.

DEAR MARK: *Besides card counters, have any other players ever been barred from playing blackjack based on certain strategies?* **Melvin D.**

I really can't answer for every casino on why, or if, they would heave-ho a player based on playing strategies, Melvin, but how about being banned for having too much capital? It happened when Australian billionaire Kerry Packer beat the MGM in Las Vegas out of $26 million, most of it while playing blackjack. The casino finally barred him, not because he was a card counter but because he was more capitalized than the casino.

When you put together a lucky streak and a player with more financial resources than the house, you've got a possibility of casino closure—permanently.

DEAR MARK: *What is the worst move a player can make with a hand while playing blackjack?* **Susan L.**

Getting ridiculous here, Susan, it's actions like doubling down on a natural blackjack. Actually I've seen this done once with a $200 wager where alcohol got the best of this party animal. Now for the average player in the casino, it's standing on a pair of eights versus a dealer upcard of 7 instead of splitting them. A player making this basic strategy error will lose 70% of the time.

Susan, you are the type of player who always plays perfect basic strategy, right?

DEAR MARK: *Last year when I went to see the dolphin exhibit at the Mirage in Las Vegas and it was just $3. Now they are asking more than triple that. What gives?* **Henry P.**

I've got a sneaky suspicion that Steve Wynn, owner of Mirage Resorts, recently changed toothpaste's to one that contains those extra whitening ingredients. You need a cunning pearly white smile when you dupe patrons who once paid $3 to view the hotel's captive dolphins to now fork over ten bucks—although he threw in a few white tigers as a bonus. Whoopee!

The point I'm trying to make here is that if you're coming to Las Vegas, you better be prepared to spend moocho dinero. Bargain lodging and $2.49 prison chow buffets are becoming an endangered genera.

With more than 40% of the total revenues on the Strip now coming from non-casino sources—and growing five times as fast as the casino take—plan on casino operators reaching into your wallet for any, and every, thing they can.

"There is plenty of time to win this game, and to thrash the Spaniards too." – SIR FRANCIS DRAKE

♠ 26 ♠
Playing Bingo can
be Sound Gambling

DEAR MARK: *Horrific as it sounds, it seems that the only game I'm able to win at lately is bingo. The thing is, for a comparatively small amount of money I can get a pretty good return. It also makes a nice relaxing change of pace if I'm on a losing streak and need to slow down my losses but I just don't want to leave the casino yet. Agree?* **Rick M.**

Most players don't realize it, but bingo is one game the casino offers that generally operates as a loss-leader for the house. Casinos can actually show a net loss by paying out more in guaranteed prizes than they take in. Now for those who think $5 is a hefty price for a buy-in, try a special non-cash game—yes, FREE—that casinos occasionally advertise.

Rick, you answered your own question correctly. Bingo does offer a great return and is a nice, relaxing change of pace if you're on a losing streak and need to slow down your losses.

DEAR MARK: *I am planning my first trip to Las Vegas. The only game I play is Video Poker. Any recommendations on where to play?* **Annie C.**

One of the great things about playing video poker, Annie, is that the casino actually tells you which machines are better than others. How? Just by reading the paytable displayed on the machine's faceplate. So who has the best paytables in Las Vegas? Have your cabby drop you off at the Stratosphere. By offering "certified" 100+ payouts on quarter machines, the Stratosphere may very well be, according to their claim, "the best place to gamble on the planet."

My personal favorites are their 10/6 and 9/7 Jacks or Better machines. With perfect play, the 10/6 machine will return 100.7 percent and the 9/7 machine 100.8 percent. Throw in some slot club card perks, Annie, and the Stratosphere is actually paying you to gamble.

51

DEAR MARK: *How do you judge one casino as being better than another?* **Missy D.**

Tastes will always vary, Missy, but when I'm asked which is "the best" casino to play in, I'm particular. Yes, a casino offering a 99¢ breakfast special is enticing, a $3.49 prime rib buffet tempting, a comp to a Broadway musical is worth kissing up to a pit boss for, but my answer will always remain the same. I judge a casino "the best" by where gaming rules maximize a players chances of winning.

Examples: Single versus double zeros on a roulette table; blackjack dealt from a single deck with liberal rules like doubling on anything, resplitting and surrender; a crap game offering five or ten times odds in lieu of two-times odds; a mini-baccarat table with low limits; casinos that advertise 98.5% paybacks on their slot machines, then tell you which machines those are when you ask; and finally, my favorite, 9/6 video poker machines.

The other casinos? They can keep their 49¢ hot dogs and free coffee mugs. I suggest that if you're willing to find "the best" casino my way, you will have a much better chance of winning. And isn't that what we're really there for?

DEAR MARK: *Who has the best shrimp cocktail in Las Vegas?* **Tom T.**

I'm partial to a joint downtown called the Golden Gate. They're cheap (99¢), have no filler (generally 50 percent celery), and the servings are huge. You'll find these bargain shrimp cocktails in the deli near the rear of the casino.

I'll be in Las Vegas next month to field-test these denizens of the deep, again, for the tenth time, to make sure I'm not giving out erroneous information.

♠ 27 ♠
The Name is Bond, James Bond

DEAR MARK: *You answered a question by stating that the most popular number played on a roulette wheel was 17 and reasoned that this was so because it was located in the center of the layout and everyone could reach it. I guess my point is that it is likely that other factors add to the "appeal" of 17 for the masses. I suggest that its popularity is based somewhat on the James Bond films where he bets "17 Black." Just a hunch, but I know many players who bet this way.* **Jimmy H.**

Correct you are, Jimmy. Bond did enjoy both baccarat and roulette as a way to relax and unwind after saving the world. And yes, players drinking martinis, shaken not stirred, tend to follow his pattern of play.

Besides birthday and anniversary dates, many players choose numbers used in the movies, from record LPs (the Beatles; number 9, number 9, number 9), even after a player's favorite athlete. Popular in northern Nevada when I dealt the game was 16 Red, Joe Montana's jersey number and color.

Getting back to Her Majesty's favorite secret agent: The most popular number in the movies is not 17, even if it was a favorite of Ian Fleming's Bond, but 22. You'll see it played at pivotal points in "Casablanca," "The Sting" and "Lost in America."

Also of little note, 22, my personal favorite, was the first number called at Bill's Casino at south Lake Tahoe when it officially opened on July 1, 1987 at 7:01 p.m. And who (brag mode ON) called that first number? Yours truly (brag mode OFF). One player had a $25 chip on it and won $875.

DEAR MARK: *I am having a minor dispute with a friend about 'jack's or better' five card draw.*

Is there usually (obviously house rules vary from place to place, but in general) a requirement to prove you have a pair of jacks or better to open? When I learned this game, there was no such requirement and you could actually bluff the open. My friend now tells me that this is not the case and penalties like matching the pot are usually imposed if the opener does bluff. What is your experience on this issue? **John K.**

When I was growing up, John, if I misplayed a hand in pinochle, fraudulently or not, the chastening was not only getting the heave-ho from the game but castigated for piss-poor play and an additional penalty of washing all the dishes. This is how I learned that honesty prevails in card play. But I'm writing about a friendly, or in my case, a hostile game environment at the kitchen table where local rules apply.

In casino poker rooms, they don't offer a jack's or better game for one simple reason. SHOW ME THE MONEY! Casinos can't pay the lighting bills on the many dead hands that a Jack's or better game would create. You can't 'rake' a pot that isn't there. The rake, the money that the card room charges, is usually a percentage or flat fee taken from the pot after each round of betting. Every time a dealer pitches out a hand, your miserly casino owner wants a piece of the action.

As for home rules, I've heard of everything from matching the pot to forfeiting the hand, and in a worst case senerio, the bucking up for all the booze and burgers.

So in the future, John, let whoever is gracious enough to let you spill beer and chip dip all over their carpet make the rules of the house.

"Baccarat is a game whereby the croupier gathers in money with a flexible sculling oar, then rakes it home. If I could have borrowed his oar I would have stayed." – MARK TWAIN

♠ 28 ♠
Dealers Call These Players...

DEAR MARK: *I hate gambling with my cousin. Not only is he irritating to other players on the table, he is very abusive to the dealer. You have no idea how many times the dealer has to tell him, could you please do this, don't do that. How about some written table manners I can pass his way?* **Janie T.**

A front-line employee of a casino, Janie, must obey two rules when it comes to customers—even your cousin. One, the player is always right, and two, if the player is wrong, see rule number one. Not easy when a decent percentage of players are running on high octane drinks and losing money. And though Bozo players (what we would call your cousin) get their fair share of negative commentary in the employee breakroom, a dealer who lashes out at any customer would be severely reprimanded—fired!

But me, I've been paroled from my 18-year casino sentence, so I can dole out some table etiquette without repercussion. Here goes.

• Know the proper hit/stand signals for the blackjack game you're playing.
• In baseball, it's two hand for beginners; on a live blackjack game, the opposite. Some casinos are real touchy-feely (throw you out) about you doing anything funny to the cards.
• Once you've placed your wager, don't touch your bet until you get paid.
• If the cards are running against you, don't keep asking for a new deck.
• If you don't like your cards, move to another table.
• Expect with abusive language an early departure from the casino.
• Don't ask the dealer what her hole card is. Dealers won't risk their job over your wager. There's nothing wrong with asking for advice, but not after the dealer looks under her face/ace.

55

- If you lose several hands in a row, don't accuse the dealer of cheating. Most (99.999%) don't. It's most likely a bad run of cards plus let's not discount poor play. Also, abusing "the messenger" for crummy cards lacks any form of civility.
- If you're using a basic strategy card (recommended), don't refer to it each and every hand. You should have a basic understanding on how to play most of your hands well before you sit down on a game.
- Using these lines? "Are you going to be nice to me?" Question is, are you going to be nice to them. "Where are you from?" It's most likely on their nametag. "Do you live here?" Yes, we're not Martians commuting from Mars. Try some other light conversation. Note: About every recipe I know, from avocado dip to chicken wings, came from some customer.
- Don't walk up to a dealer and tell him he looks bored, make him shuffle a 6-deck shoe just to play one $5 bet, lose, then walk.
- When betting for the dealer (worth at least three separate columns), keep the ratio a reasonable one. I once viewed a professional baseball player betting three hands at $500 a whack, with just a 50¢ bet for the dealer, every third shuffle. One month earlier he signed a multi-million-dollar, 5-year contract. His initials are…. I better not.
- Once the hand has been completed, don't turn your cards over to help the dealer. Dealers have a routine and you're just slowing them down. Besides, dealers need to spread the cards a certain way so the cameras can read them.

Finally, dealers really don't care if the sign outside their casino says "certified friendly dealers." They just want to be treated like you would want to be treated.

♠ 29 ♠
Buffets are a Nevada State Treasure

DEAR MARK: *I enjoy going to Las Vegas not only to gamble but to feast on all the different buffets. Why do you think they don't offer buffets with the same fanfare in the Midwest casinos as they do in Las Vegas?* **Chuck M.**

On those days, Chuck, when you have to try as hard as you can to keep up with the losers, your only salvation is to get up from a losing table and enjoy the comfort cuisine of a rich bounty buffet.

Casinos here have long realized that the formula for success in a casino is to attract as many people as possible, with the least amount of marketing costs, and keep them in their facility for as long as they have money in their pocket. A buffet is one of the best ways of doing that. The Rio Hotel and Casino in Las Vegas is a perfect example of a casino whose tremendous success is rooted in its Carnival World Buffet.

Why the chow-line dining experience hasn't caught on at all the heartland casinos, where eating quantity over quality has always prevailed, is beyond my grasp.

DEAR MARK: *When making a bet on the "bank hand" in baccarat, why do they charge a 5% commission? Wouldn't this make it an inferior wager compared to a "player hand" bet?* **Bradley G.**

Based on the mathematics of baccarat, the player hand should win 44.6% of the time, the bank hand 45.8% and the tie 9.6%. If we discount ties, the player hand statistically will win 49.3% of the time and the bank hand 50.7%.

Because the bank hand wins more than 50% of the time, the casino neutralizes this edge you would have over the house by charging a 5% commission every time you win a bank hand bet. By charging this hidden tax, the casino's advantage is now 1.17% for bank hand and 1.36% for the player hand. But even with the commission added, you can see that the bank hand is still a slightly better bet than the player wager.

By the way, Bradley, the above wagers are some of the best bets you can make in a casino, but the tie bet should always be avoided: house edge, 14.1%.

DEAR MARK: *I understand most of the logic behind basic strategy, but one play always makes me nervous and that is doubling down on a 10 against a dealer's 10. If I assume the dealer has a total of 20, then only a ten card or ace will allow me to win. Am I right to assume that there are more chances I'll draw a 2-9 card than a 10 or ace? If so, why double my bet in such a risky situation?* **Allen H.**

Blackjack is a game in which the proper hit, stand, splitting and doubling decisions are necessary to cut the house edge down to a minimum. These proper decisions are called basic strategy and have been arrived at by computer simulations of millions of hands.

Your case in point, doubling down on a 10 against a dealer 10 is NOT one of those times. Basic strategy dictates you hit your hand, not double down. This stratagem is the same for both single and multiple deck games.

DEAR MARK: *You have mentioned in previous columns both your favorite books and movies on gambling. Do you have any favorite songs on gambling?* **Stathis Z.**

Hmmm. A beloved song on gambling. Yes I do. Two actually. *There's A Place in the World for A Gambler* by pop singer Dan Fogelberg and *Luck be a Lady* by Frank Sinatra.

There's a place in the world for a gambler
There's a burden that only he can bare
There's a place in the world for a gambler
And he sees
Oh yes he sees.

♠ 30 ♠
What's the Deal and Appeal
with Caribbean Stud

DEAR MARK: *In the past, individuals have written you asking specific questions about Caribbean Stud Poker. Could you please give a brief explanation of how the game is played, its downside and is it really as popular as everyone says?* **Donald B.**

The basic objective of this five-card stud poker game is to beat the dealer's hand. To play, you must first place an ante bet in the circle. Let's use a $5 ante wager as our example. You then receive five cards dealt face down, and the dealer gets four cards face down and one card exposed. If you feel your 5 cards can beat the dealer's hand, you then place an additional bet equaling twice your ante ($10). Otherwise, you fold and lose your original $5. All that remains is beating the dealer's hand and you win! Well, not so fast my friend.

If the dealer doesn't have at least a king plus an ace to open, all you win is even money on your $5 ante wager. True, there is a bonus payout schedule for hands ranging from one pair to a royal flush when the dealer's hand is in play, but when I've got 15 buckaroos on the table at risk, I want a $15 payoff if the dealer is forced to fold. There, Donald, is your downside.

As for its popularity, Donald, no argument from me that Caribbean Stud is one of the fastest growing table games today. Many players believe the attractive payback percentage and the added thrill of a progressive jackpot is just too hard to resist. But smart gamblers—those who stick with wagers that have less than a 2% house advantage—realize the house wins two ways: off the basic game percentage (5.3%) and as a percentage return (48%) of the popular progressive bet.

DEAR MARK: *My mother and I just discovered the joys of playing bingo at an Indian reservation. Our problem is that if we play more than two cards at one time, we're overwhelmed. Any suggestions?* **Marion E.**

Save the mind labor, Marion, and join the cybernetic age. Most Indian reservation bingo parlors rent out computers (for a nominal price) that automatically track up to 12 bingo cards at one time. When a number is called, you one-touch a video bingo screen, and a computer searches for the number on all your cards, then imprints the correct spot for the game theme or pattern you are playing.

For the laggards like yours truly, it's heaven sent.

DEAR MARK: *I can't wait for gambling to come to Detroit. Do you think with just three casinos, there will be enough competition to benefit the player?* **Benny D.**

A resounding NO, and here's why. The precipitous price for those three casino licensees will have to be absorbed by the unwilling and unknowing player. For starters, a state gaming tax of 18 percent of the casino profits was set by Michigan's Proposition E referendum. Next, add an additional $25 million a year to the Michigan Gaming Control Board, plus $5 million for compulsive gambling. State legislators also enacted laws that require each licensee to pay more than $8 million in annual fees. As the Consumer Price Index increases, so do the service fees. The casinos must also pay an additional annual municipal fee of 1.25 percent of the adjusted gross receipts, or $4 million, whichever is greater.

Now if you think the Lords of Chance will be footing the bill for the price of a casino license—the highest amount extracted yet from any casino operator—lose the tears. They'll sulk like a 10-year-old when they have to fork over so much money, but whose pocket will they really take it out of? YOURS. How? By oppressive rules in blackjack, sky-high limits at table games, tight video poker machines and even tighter cybernetic one-armed bandits.

Welcome, Detroit, my hometown, to what I believe will be some of the highest table limits and toughest odds nationwide. For the customers' sake, I hope I'm wrong and will have to digest these words.

♠ 31 ♠
My Favorite Cee-ment Ponds

DEAR MARK: *My sister and I love to spend the day by the pool before we take in a little gambling in the evening. Since we are going to Las Vegas next month, do you have any recommendations of hotels that offer decent pools?* **Faye K,**

Congratulations, Faye, for treating gambling more like a time-killing recreational activity. All gamblers when coming to Las Vegas should plan other activities like visiting the Hoover Dam, the many fine shows, shopping, health clubs, tennis or golf. Make it an enjoyable, entertaining trip, not all gambling.

Now for my favorite cee-ment ponds. I'll first preface my choices by telling you that gray is my favorite color, and I love inclement weather, not the heat or intense sunshine of Las Vegas. But since you asked, my preferred choices, for all the wrong reasons, are the swimming holes at the Rio, the Mirage and the Tropicana: the Rio, not because they actually have a sandy beach, but because it's closest to my favorite buffet; the Mirage, not because it's the place to be seen, but because I kept a room key from a previous visit so when my friends stay in Vegas I can sneak in; and finally, the Tropicana, not because it has the largest pool or poolside blackjack, but because if you walk up to the Island Winners Club, fill out a player application, and gamble a minimal amount, they'll give you a room for $39.95.

So based on what you just read, Faye, you really don't want my opinion. Instead, call the Las Vegas Chamber for hotel information at (800) 445-8864 and see what they recommend.

DEAR MARK: *Why is it that every time the dice fly off the table, the next number to roll is the seven? Uncanny isn't it? Should I bet on the seven every time the dice go off the game?* **Robert N.**

You would think, Robert, that every time you hear a dealer call "It's on the ground, look around, it must be found" or "Too tall to call" that the smart thing to do would be to place a wager on the number seven because you believe it's going to roll again. You'd be thinkin' wrong, pardner.

By making this wager part of your betting repertoire, you could easily be joining the most pathetic bunch of losers since my ninth grade remedial shop math class. Why? Because the probability of a seven showing on any roll, off the table or not, is only 16.67 percent. Forget what you perceive. Each roll of the dice always remains the same, an independent event. More bad news. The one-roll wager on the seven is the worst bet on the crap table. Casino advantage, 16.7 percent.

Sorry, Robert, what you perceive as happening all the time is anecdotal evidence, not reality. Stay away from this wager!

DEAR MARK: *I love the thrill and action of a casino. My wife, out of fear of making mistakes and being harassed by other players, prefers to sit in front of a slot machine. She avoids table games like the plague. I can't even get her to play with me on my favorite game, blackjack. Do many players have this anxiety?* **Chuck L.**

Anyone who has ever been chastised for hitting a 16 when the dealer shows a five can appreciate the anonymity of a slot machine. Your wife obviously prefers a non-threatening environment where her decisions won't be second-guessed.

I'm with you, Chuck. I would love to see your wife experience table games offering excellent bets for the player, but who can blame her? Why get verbally abused for faulty draws when a slot machine will allow her the freedom to play her way, at her own pace, without harassment.

"The difference between wagering and commerce lies neither in pleasure nor in profit, but in the amount of social stigma attached to the process."
– RICHARD SASULY, GAMBLING HISTORIAN

♠ 32 ♠
Las Vegas is Cheapskate City

DEAR MARK: *I received an advertisement in the mail that offered a book of coupons that I can use on my next trip to Las Vegas. They wanted $4.95 for $200 worth of coupons. Is that a good deal?* **Terry C.**

Save your money, Terry. Not only is Las Vegas the hot dog and shrimp cocktail capital of the world, but for the coupon clipper, Las Vegas is the "half-off" city. Everywhere you look, or go, newsstands will be loaded with, and hawkers passing out, coupons with the latest bargains in Las Vegas. The favorite of many who journey to Vegas is *What's On in Las Vegas.* With a 130,000-per-issue circulation, you will find this FREE, coupon-laden publication everywhere.

I'll be forthcoming here, Terry. I'm a big time tightwad. I won't, nor should you, pay full price for anything.

DEAR MARK: *I have two blackjack questions for you. First, what is the house advantage, if any, if I use a never-bust system against the dealer? Also, is it better to play on a blackjack game where the dealer hits a soft 17 or stands?* **Thomas D.**

Over the years I've seen many losing players employ this never-bust strategy. Right off the top, they're giving the house a 5% edge. Strict basic strategy, which obviously recommends hitting plenty of stiff hands, cuts the house edge to a half of one percent on the six-or eight-deck games that you'll find in the Chicago area. Use it, or plan on losing it—all.

When you play a game in which the dealer hits a soft 17, you give the house an additional two-tenths of one percent. With a soft 17 showing, an Ace, 2, 3 or 4 improves the dealer's hand and a 10, Jack, Queen or King leaves it of equivalent value. Eight of every 13 cards, Thomas, either improves the dealers hand or it stays the same. If any of the other five cards are drawn, the dealer still has a chance to convalesce his hand with another draw.

For the above reason, Thomas, basic strategy dictates that you the player should always hit a soft 17, or double down against a dealer who's showing a 3, 4, 5, 6.

DEAR MARK: *Could you please give a brief description of the rules for Let It Ride?* **Hugh G.**

Let It Ride is based on the all-American game of five-card stud poker. The game begins with every player placing three equal wagers on their individual betting circles. The object of the game is to get a winning poker hand (10s or better) using your three cards plus the dealers two "community" cards. Your three cards are dealt face down, and the two community cards are placed face down in front of the dealer.

After looking at your three cards, you may ask to have your bet returned or "let it ride," depending on whether your cards show the possibility of a winning hand. Then the dealer's first community card is turned over, and again you can ask for your bet back or let it ride. Finally, the second community card is turned over, completing both the player's poker hand and the game. Your third bet, a contract wager, is committed to play and can't be returned. The dealer then pays all the winning hands according to a payout schedule. The higher the rank hand, the greater the payoff, with a royal flush paying 1,000 to one.

The game is fairly simple, Hugh, but because 70% of the hands are outright losers, the house edge (3.5%) is well above my recommended maximum of 2%. I recommend you stick with some of the better bets that the casino has to offer.

"You know what luck is? Luck is believing you're lucky...to hold front position in this rat-race you've got to believe you're lucky." – STANLEY KOWALSKI, A STREETCAR NAMED DESIRE

♠ 33 ♠
Do Casinos Cheat?

DEAR MARK: *I have always been a bit suspicious of casinos and especially their ability to cheat players. Come clean, Mark. Do the casinos tell the dealers to cheat the customer?* **Ron T.**

If you follow my column regularly, Ron, you will notice my commentary ordinarily puts me on the side of the player. With machete in hand, I am always willing to slash through the green felt jungle for my readers. Most would call me a casino adversary/player advocate. Thank you. But in the case of a casino cheating a player, Ron, I would be remiss if I didn't say with 100 percent conviction that the casinos are in no way out to cheat you.

There are two key reasons why casinos don't play the game of deception. First, most casinos are publicly traded companies on the NYSE not interested in exposing their gaming license to loss with any inkling of cheating going on. Also, here in Nevada, you won't find a more regulated industry chock-full of rules that would close a casino down for defrauding the public.

A second, if not even more significant reason, is the way casinos reap their profits—paying players less than the true odds. Meaning, every game offered to the player is mathematically in the casino's favor. Example: When you flip a coin there is a 50/50 chance of your winning. But instead of getting even money for every dollar you wager, you are paid 99¢, or 83¢ or maybe even 75¢. This in a nutshell is how casinos operate their license to print money, paying you less than even money on every bet you make.

Now, if every single wager placed in the casino is based on that principle, why, Ron, would they ever want to swindle you? That's not to say that a rogue employee on his own never tries to manipulate the cards in the casino's favor. That is why the casino manager watches the shift manager, who watches the pit bosses, who watches the floorman, who watches the dealers—with the eye in the sky (camera in the ceiling) watching everybody. It doesn't take long for a dishonest employee to be weeded out.

65

I would also note that in 18 years of casino employment, working in seven different casinos, I have never been asked to do even the slightest thing that borders on fraud. I have been asked to speed up my hands per hour dealing blackjack or pick up the pace on a crap game, but that's to get the math to work in the casino's favor never to cheat.

So, Ron, I would be more suspicious of the wagers you make, not the casino. Let me ask you this: Are you getting back 75¢ (keno) for every dollar bet, or 99¢, (perfect basic strategy in blackjack)?

Follow up: This past week I was deluged with calls and e-mail about an investigative report by ABC-TV's *PrimeTime* regarding slot machines in Nevada that are preprogrammed for "near-miss" read-outs, which entice gamblers to play longer. The theme of the discourse was "I knew all along they were cheating us."

PrimeTime's main source; a former Nevada Gaming Control Board computer whiz and convicted felon named Ron Harris, who prior to sentencing found religion.

Sorry, but I'll stick with my biased conviction that because casinos have the percentages working for them on each and every slot, there is little chance they would conspire, in this case with a slot manufacturer, to cheat a patron. All pulls of the slot handle produce random results—albeit results that, based on the slot pay table, generally create losers. Besides, near-miss technology is not only illegal in Nevada, but tampering with a computer chip can easily be detected with the right equipment, even by a low-level computer nerd like me. Chips are not only tested before leaving the factory but randomly checked for integrity on the casino floor.

Coincidentally, another TV news magazine program, to which I promised confidentiality for both the show's name and content, wanted my opinion about an upcoming investigative report they were doing regarding a highly sensitive casino issue. Because my take on the subject matter wasn't the sensationalist spin that would improve their ratings, my viewpoint will find it's way to the cutting room's floor. Why should they use me? In the gambling industry they can easily find someone with limited credentials willing to say off camera or in silhouette, "Yeah, that's the norm, happens all the time." Sounds very similar to the *PrimeTime* investigative piece above.

♠ 34 ♠
Treat Casino Chips as Your Hard Earned money

DEAR MARK: *Why is it that when I bet real cash instead of swapping for chips, I'm frowned on by the casino?* **Gerry G.**

A casino goal, Gerry, is to create a fantasyland experience for its patrons. One wily way is to devalue your money by having you bet chips instead of legal tender. Think of the deceptive nicknames chips have. A $5 chip is a "nickel" and a $25 chip a "quarter." Your best self-defense is to continue to bet with your own greenback. This way you'll always realize its genuine value.

If you do turn your bankroll into chips, take a moment and carefully think about the exchange. You must always treat chips as hard-earned cash—like the money you save for your child's college tuition, mortgage payments or your retirement.

DEAR MARK: *Almost every weekend I visit the casinos in Joliet. My brother-in-law believes they tighten the slot machines on weekends because the crowds are much larger. How do I know for sure that a casino won't change the return on their machines.* **Dirk C.**

Fear not, Dirk. Illinois, having rigid gaming regulations, requires two keys just to open a slot machine. One is held by a casino employee, the other by a state gaming regulator. This prevents changes in a machine's payout rate.

DEAR MARK: *After reading a recent column of yours, I've realized that I've been making the worst possible bet on the roulette table. Furthermore, you also educated me on looking for a single zero roulette wheel on my next trip to Las Vegas. But how much was I giving away to the casino on the five number bet before you helped me see the light?* **Wrongdoer**

Dear Wrongdoer (Lessons Learned would be a nicer name): The five number bet you were placing, 0/00/1/2/3 pays 7 for 1, with a return of .9211 on the dollar, or a house edge of 7.89%. Glad I could help you see the light.

DEAR MARK: *What is the value of doubling down on a blackjack game? Am I not exposing additional money which I could lose to the casino?* **Ross S.**

Sorry, Ross, I'm a huge fan of doubling down. Here's an opportunity where you now know what the dealer's up-card is, and the casino is allowing you to bet more money.

In blackjack, Ross, it's the natural blackjacks, splitting pairs and the ability to double down that bring your bankroll from red to black. If you're playing perfect strategy, not winging it, doubling down becomes the offensive strategy you use when the chances of winning the hand are better than the dealer's. Why? Because betting more when the casino is at a distinct disadvantage will increase your potential return more than if you were to just hit your hand.

DEAR MARK: *In many of your answers you reference 9/6 video poker machines. How do you know if a machine has a 9/6 payback? I hoped I asked that correctly?* **Sandie M.**

In earlier columns, Sandie, the message was perfect but the messenger wasn't. Ding-dong me, I sometimes forget my reading audience hasn't been in the gaming business for 18 years. Sorry.

A 9/6 payback is your return for a full house (9) and a flush (6) with one coin inserted. Your typical 9/6 Jacks-or-Better paytable will look like this:

Royal Flush	250
Straight Flush	50
Four of a Kind	25
Full House	9
Flush	6
Straight	4
Three of a Kind	3
Two Pair	2
Jacks or Better	1

And how does the casino tighten a Jacks-or-better video poker machine? Simply by paying out less for a full house and flush. This is why on a Jacks-or-better machine I ceaselessly recommend shopping for value by finding the highest payout possible for a full house and a flush.

♠ 35 ♠
Dinner in the Steakhouse
Comes with a Price

DEAR MARK: *This episode happened to me recently in Las Vegas. I was playing blackjack making $10 wagers when I was approached by a pit boss asking if there was anything he could do for me. "Sure," I replied. Can I get a dinner at the steakhouse?" His response was, "Let me track your action for a few minutes and I'll tell you what we can comp you." Well, as luck would have it, the cards weren't going my way and I left without following up on that steak dinner. But I still want to know what the pit boss meant by tracking my action for a comp?* **Stanley K.**

First, Stanley, the comp (steak dinner) is nothing more than a reward system for the worthy play of high volume players. The casino thanks you by rebating back some of your losses because you played at such a level, for such a period of time, and because they have such an advantage over you; the longer you play the more they win. So here's your carrot and please come back again.

Tracking your play means taking your average bet and multiplying it by the hours played, speed of the game and the casino advantage. This, in theory, should equal your loss.

In your case, Stanley, you mentioned betting $10 a hand. With two hour's play, averaging 100 hands per hour, coupled with the house advantage of five percent they hold over the average blackjack player, this tells Mr. Pit Boss you're going to lose $100. Because mathematically you'll lose that Ben Franklin, the casino can afford to rebate your losses in the form of a corn-fed beef dinner.

The warning here is that to give comps, the casino is going to demand action, preferably losing action. They also want you to bet a decent chunk of change for an extended period of time to justify giving you freebies.

Of course, Stanley, I always recommend grinding any comp you can get out of the casino, but I caution all players never to gamble just to receive them. It's much better to make sensible, low house advantage wagers, which will increase your winning opportunities.

DEAR MARK: *You said in a recent column that it was easier to hit my state lottery than to get a sequential royal flush. I can't be sure, but it seems I've gotten the latter but was never fortunate enough to hit the lottery. Are you sure?* **Shirley L.**

Using a software program called Statistics Menu from Spreadware, I find that the numbers crunch this way. The chances of hitting the California lottery are 18,009,460 to one. For an ascending royal flush in any suit, the chances are one in 311,875,119, a difference of elephantine proportions.

These "gimmick" bonus jackpots are nothing more than a marketing scheme to induce play. In most cases, Shirley, it's more than a challenge to win, it's impossible.

DEAR MARK: *Which slot machine revolutionized slots as we know them today?* **Jeff C.**

My answer, Jeff, will subject me to heated debate among one-armed bandit collectors— of which I'm not one—but my biased guess would be the 1964 "Money Honey" manufactured by Bally's. This machine was the first to have electronic circuitry to read the reels, a hopper, relays for protection against slot cheating and a brightly lit front end. The latter, mind you, was not for esthetics but for inducing play.

DEAR MARK: *On a recent trip to Las Vegas, I noticed a fascinating slot machine on display that was built from a wooden cowboy. As a collector of gambling artifacts, I would like to add one to my collection. Two questions: Are these machines a rarity? And who designed them?* **Stewart K.**

Scarce, yes, as only 92 were made in 1950. The ingenious cowboy artist who created the life-size human figures on slot machines was Frank Polk.

"I am sorry I have not learned to play cards. It is very useful in life. It generates kindness and consolidates society."
– SAMUEL JOHNSON

♠ 36 ♠
Your Ticket to Three Squares a Day

DEAR MARK: *I know the following question I'm about to ask is illegal, but I'm still interested. A small factory close to my home discards a circular coin-like metal that is exactly the same size and weight as the silver dollar coins used in a casino. If I were caught inserting the coins into a machine, what would happen?* **Anonymous**

This ditty written by Ian Lewis best illustrates what will befall the ignorant found inserting slugs into a casino slot machine.

"Bad boys, bad boys, whatcha gonna do, whatcha gonna do when they come for you?"

The TV show "COPS" is filmed on location in the city of Las Vegas.

DEAR MARK: *Why don't nickel machines return the same percentages as quarter machines?* **Sara R.**

The main reason nickel machines have poorer payouts than quarters, and why quarters less than dollars is because the cost to maintain any machine—slot personnel, floor space, maintenance, etc.,—is exactly the same. Each slot has to yield a targeted number of dollars for the casino, so a larger percentage must be kept from the lower denomination machines to meet those goals.

DEAR MARK: *Even when playing perfect basic strategy at blackjack where the house edge is nil, I still occasionally go home losing. Explanation please.* **Sheldon M.**

Enter Pilarski's rule number seven of gaming: "The odds are even money that the light at the end of the tunnel is the headlight of an oncoming train."

It is called gambling, Sheldon.

DEAR MARK: *Because you mentioned that slots operate using the same computer chip as a video poker machine, why not stick with slots as they are easier to play?* **Larry L.**

True, Larry, the first part of your question is correct in that most of today's video games (video poker, video blackjack and video keno) are derivatives of slot machines and actually use the same microprocessor technology and random number sequences, but, video poker, blackjack and keno machines provide players with real options and choices that require an element of skill that regular slot machines don't. With this skill, you can hack away at the high house advantage that the average slot machine holds over you.

DEAR MARK: *Why is it that you recommend learning and playing more than one type of game in a casino?* **Robert B.**

By diversifying your playing portfolio and learning different games, when you do have a run of bad luck in blackjack, you can always try craps or video poker.

DEAR MARK: *What exactly is the house edge?* **Lefty O.**

The house edge is a mathematical percentage—always in the casino's favor—that the casino takes on each bet. This edge is the casino's true income and why they can build those high rises. For the house to pay for those construction costs, winning bets are paid off at less than true odds.

Lefty, consider it a payment for playing in their establishment, or, an entertainment tax.

DEAR MARK: *A dealer once told me that the only way to "soar like an eagle" when playing baccarat is to bet ties after they appear. He claimed they always repeat in streaks. Was he correct?* **Bobby K.**

Eagles may soar, but in this case it's better to gamble like a chicken because they don't get sucked into jet engines. By betting only on the bank or player hands, Bobby, you will avoid being recycled at Foster Farms. That dealer-induced tie bets hold a house advantage of 14.1%.

As for streaks, Bobby, the remaining cards in the shoe have no memory, hence, previous results have no bearing on what happens in the future.

♠ 37 ♠
Is Counting Worth the Hassle?

DEAR MARK: *I've been kicking around the idea of becoming a blackjack card counter for years. I have decent math skills and am willing to spend time learning the game. I would like to hear some of your thoughts, theories, practical application of, advice and a brief explanation on how counting actually works. Hopefully you'll give me some inspiration to learn counting, maybe even make it a career.* **Eric G.**

Eric, you want my thoughts, advice, etc. on counting? OK, lend me your ear, but you might not like what you are about to hear.

The Player: All card counters I have met think they are the sharpest knife in the drawer. Forget dialog with them to the contrary, they all believe they can beat the house at will, any time, any place. In reality, I've found more mediocre counters than good ones, and egos larger than the casino operators. I figure the subliminal self of counters is based on abnormally high testosterone levels.

Them Guys: Working the pits for years, taking numerous seminars on counting, plus being a proficient counter myself—me make it a career move? NOT—I can smell a counter a mile away. Even your average pitboss will take simple measures to combat these casino pests. Pit bosses will hassle counters by putting more decks on the game, burying more cards on the shuffle, stopping mid-entry shoe betting, having the dealer shuffle half way through the deck, and when all else fails, back you off the game.

The Money Makers: So is anyone truly making money on card counting? Sure. A very small, select group of counters who have created a cottage industry of seminars, tapes, books and newsletters on counting. For most experts, writing about playing is more lucrative than playing itself.

Hitting the Casino: Card counters, theoretically, have an inherent advantage of between .5 and 1.5 percent against the casino. Counting theory is quite simple. Big cards (10s, aces) favor the player, small cards (2-6) favor the dealer.

All card counting systems keep track of the relationship of small cards to big cards remaining in the deck. When the cards remaining favor the player, you bet more money. When they favor the dealer, you bet less.

The simplest count to learn is a one level count, a.k.a the Hi-Lo counting system. It assigns the following count values to each card.

2, 3, 4, 5, 6 (small cards).......................+1
7, 8, 9 (neutral cards).............................. 0
10, J, Q, K, Ace (big cards)....................-1

To use the Hi-Lo method, you need to add and subtract the above counting values for every card exposed on the blackjack table. By mentally keeping an updated running count from one hand to the next, you vary your bets according to the positive/negative value of the upcoming hand.

But it all comes back to our jumpy pit boss who wants to run you out the door. He's just not going to be happy with blackjack players who know how to beat the house. He would much prefer players who think they know how to win but are experts at losing—players on the bottom rung of the casino food chain.

Geez, Eric, I'm just warming up, but because of limited space I'm forced to come full circle. If you're still going to make card counting a career move, may I make a final suggestion? Don't quit your day job.

DEAR MARK: *If in all blackjack scenarios you should hit a soft 17 (A-6), why would you never hit a hard 17?* **Jim T.**

Unfortunately, Jim, a 17 in blackjack is a damned hand, a dud over the long haul. The alternative strategy of hitting a hard 17 would only multiply your losses. Nevertheless, with a soft 17 you at least have the possibility of taking another card, which could improve your hand. This is why basic strategy charts dictate either hitting or doubling down, never standing on a soft 17.

"The race is not to the swift, nor the battle to the strong, nor bread to the wise, nor riches to the intelligent...but time and chance happen to them all." – ECCLESIASTES 9:11

♠ 38 ♠
Some Do's and Don'ts Before Your Trip to Las Vegas

DEAR MARK: *Next month I am flying to Las Vegas for the first time. Not only is it my first trip to Nevada but also my first visit to a casino. Any do's and don'ts you could recommend before I go?* **Mary S.**

Here are some *do's* and *don'ts*, Mary, that everyone should know before they make their first flight to the mothership, Las Vegas. Learn them, live by them, and your casino experience can be very rewarding.

First, *do* decide ahead of time which games you are going to play and for what stakes.

Do plan other activities like shows, shopping, sightseeing, the health club or golf. Make it an enjoyable, entertaining trip, not all gambling.

Do comparison shop for the best buys on meals and accommodations. Also, *do* comparison shop for bargains on the best rules and playing conditions for the particular games you're going to be playing.

Do monitor the status of your bankroll. At all times you should know where you are financially.

Do count your blessings. If you break even your first time gambling, that's a win in anybody's book.

Do check the many Las Vegas gambling guides found at newspaper stands for the best values and deals.

Finally, *do* keep up to date on both rule changes and different variations of your favorite game because casinos can, and will, change the rules all the time. The winning player is always the informed player.

On the flip side, Mary, honoring these *don'ts* should put you in a position of gambling without tears.

Don't bet over your head but only with what you can afford to lose.

Don't play with scared money.

Don't borrow money from friends to finance your gambling or try to recoup your losses.

Don't press your bets if you're on a losing streak.

Don't be superstitious. Knowledge is the key, not luck. Like I've said many times in this column: "The smarter you play, the luckier you'll be."

Don't waste your time on games or wagers where the casino has a house advantage of more than 2%.

Don't play any game or make any bet you know little about. Learn it first.

Don't drink excessively and gamble at the same time. Sip for pleasure, don't gulp for effect.

Don't be afraid to ask questions. Who's money is it? YOURS.

Don't be greedy. Be satisfied with a small win.

The above suggestions, Mary, should make your pilgrimage to the Mecca of gambling all that more enjoyable.

DEAR MARK: *Do you, as an informed video poker player, ever ignore the strict rules of basic strategy?* **Jenny S.**

The correct answer should be, NO, not me, NEVER. Basic strategy charts are derived not from some slick huckster selling his latest beat-the-casino system but by mathematicians and countless computer studies.

But, Jenny, I'll come clean here. There is one hand in which I completely disregard the correct betting approach. When dealt a high pair along with three cards to the royal, I say, the hell with basic strategy.

The research conducted by high-priced computer scientists tells you to keep the high pair. I go for the royal flush every time. The additional strength (expected value) of a high pair hand versus three cards to a royal is so negligible, I always jump on the chance, as remote as it might be, of hitting the elusive royal flush.

DEAR MARK: *Who controls the payback of a slot machine, the slot manufacturer or the casino?* **Jim K.**

Today's slot machines contain a random number generator (RNG) that controls the payback percentage of each machine. When a casino purchases a slot machine it tells the manufacturer what percentage it wants that particular machine to return to its customers. That amount is pre-programmed into the RNG at the plant. A casino can always change the payback percentage, but it must go back to the manufacturer and have them reprogram the RNG.

♠ 39 ♠
Winners, Not Losers,
Pay the Electric Bills

DEAR MARK: *I've heard from other individuals and read from you about the "house edge" when it comes to certain casino games. So, if you wouldn't mind, can you explain to me how the house advantage on a roulette table is determined?* **Michael K.**

The casino's edge or advantage is different from game to game and from the distinct wagers on those games.

The best way to understand the concept of the casino advantage is to think of it as a hidden tax when you win a bet, NOT when you lose your wager. Yes, Michael, you are reading this correctly! It is when you win that the casino reaches for your wallet. By not receiving a fair payout for a winning wager, you are charged this secret levy that you probably don't realize you're paying.

In roulette, a fair payout on a $1 winning number is $37. However, the casino only pays you $35. It retains the extra $2, giving the house its 5.26% advantage. It is that $2 into the casino's coffers that gives the casino its profits.

Your goal as a smart casino player is to lessen this concealed charge. By reducing the casino advantage with bets that carry a low house edge, you will minimize your losses and have a much better chance of winning.

DEAR MARK: *I played a game called Bayou BlackJack in Louisiana where the dealer shows both of his cards before you take your first hit. Do you know where this game is played in Las Vegas?* **Hal G.**

A place you don't want to be. Also called Double Exposure black-jack, this is yet another variation of blackjack in which the rule changes are not always in the player's best interest. The biggest modification from conventional blackjack is that both the dealer cards are dealt face-up. However, because you view both of the dealer's up-cards, the playing rules are adjusted to favor the casino more than standard blackjack. This includes paying blackjacks at even money, doubling down permitted only on 9, 10, 11; and insurance, re-splits and surrender are not allowed. Also, all tie hands result in a loss with the exception of a player's blackjack. It beats a dealer's snapper.

Because of these rule changes, Hal, Bayou Blackjack is not as auspicious as traditional casino blackjack. It's a game worth avoiding.

DEAR MARK: *Are there any advantages to playing on a video blackjack machine versus a live action game?* **P. J.**

Sure, if you split 10s against a dealer 6 on a video game, no fellow player can verbally violate you.

Seriously, unless you find a machine that pays you the true value of a blackjack (3 for 2), look at most video blackjack machines with a jaundiced eye. Most machines pay even money on natural 21s. Because you can expect a snapper every 21 hands in live play, the loss of that bonus will cost you an additional 2.3 percent. Considering that blackjack has a house advantage of less than .5 percent to a knowledgeable player, you are giving away the farm here.

Other machines round down on blackjack payoffs. If you do happen to find a machine that pays the bonus for a blackjack, make wagers in even amounts so you can get the maximum value of a blackjack (a pay-off of $3 for every $2 wagered). And what will a dollar wagered get you for a blackjack? Just a buck, so always bet in two-unit increments.

The advantage of a video blackjack machine vs. a live game is the low minimum bankroll requirement needed to play. I've seen 5¢ and many 25¢ video blackjack games on the casino floor. They also lack the intimidation factor of a live game, plus they make excellent practice session mates where you can work on perfect basic strategy.

♠ 40 ♠
How Much is Enough?

DEAR MARK: *I work as a dealer on an Indian reservation in northern Michigan. One of the most common mistakes I see is players getting ahead, then giving all their winnings back to the casino. Why do you think so many players are boneheads?* **Anonymous for job protection.**

One word, GREED. Too many players, when greed sets in, keep upping the ante on what they want to win. "Enough" is just over the horizon, and like the horizon, it recedes when they approach it.

This column always recommends having a predetermined win plan. All players should set loss limits and win goals. Without this money management strategy, your typical player generally becomes a casino statistic called the "hold," a percentage of chips purchased by the customer and then won back by the casino. All too often, when the rapacity of a player goes unchecked, the player's entire bankroll slowly but surely reverts to the casino.

DEAR MARK: *If a slot machine pays back with hot coins, does that mean it's a hot machine?* **Sly G.**

No, Sly, the temperature of the coins has nothing to do with the machine's payback percentage.

I remember years ago seeing a gentleman heating up his coins with a hair dryer in the men's bathroom. In questioning his gaming prowess he replied with unwavering conviction that inserting hot coins produced more winners because the coins coming out of his favorite machine were hot. My explanation that coins falling out hot is due to the close proximity of lights and other electrical components to the hopper fell on deaf ears.

79

DEAR MARK: *Is there any difference between the crap tables of Nevada and those in Atlantic City?* **William B.**

Excluding the ability in Nevada to take higher odds on your line bets, the biggest difference on the craps table layout in Atlantic City is there is no *big 6 or 8.* When the player bets on the *big 6 or 8,* the payoff is even money, whereas it is 7-to-6 bet when either the 6 or 8 is wagered as a "place bet" in either state. The latter is a much smarter wager.

DEAR MARK: *I always feel awkward when I see a player playing alone at blackjack and I want to play on the same game. What do you suggest?* **Robin W.**

When I see a player playing solo, especially when his bet exceeds what I plan on wagering, I ask him politely if he prefers to play head-to-head with the dealer or would he mind some company. This always seems to work.

DEAR MARK: *I buy $50 worth of lottery tickets per week. How long will it take for me mathematically to finally hit the jackpot?* **Jenny S.**

If, just if, Jenny, your genetic structure is predisposed to longevity, you can plan on winning the jackpot once every 7,000 years. Then again, given enough opportunity ($50 per week), any supernatural occurrence due to chance can happen. This is what makes the lottery/gambling so attractive.

DEAR MARK: *I recently found your column on an internet site in Stockholm, Sweden. I enjoy your historic questions the most. I am doing a research paper at the University about the introduction of casino gambling in the state where you live, Nevada. Can you tell me when it became a legal enterprise?* **Stefan F.**

A buckaroo politician for Humboldt County named Phil Tobin presented the assembly bill in 1931 making gambling both legal and taxable. Governor Fred Balzar, also known as "Friendly Fred," signed the open gambling law on March 19, 1931. Coincidentally, on that same day Balzar signed into law a bill that would drive tourism, he thought, far more than gambling ever would: the six weeks divorce statute.

♠ 41 ♠
Sometimes Casinos Can't Figure

DEAR MARK: *I recently received a flyer in the mail from a casino showing some of their current specials. One was being paid 2 to 1 for blackjacks on Wednesdays. A good deal for the player?* **Louise J.**

Geez, Louise, I just love it when the marketing department of a casino makes the rules. They may, or may not have known it, but when that casino decided as a promotion that it will pay you 2 to 1 for a blackjack versus 3 to 2, by God, they gave you an edge over the house. How much? Well if you played perfect basic strategy on a $5 game, you'll gain an extra $2.50 once every 20.7 hands. That's an improvement of 12 cents a hand—enough for some extra greenback in your wallet and a cheap buffet as well. But what's most important here, Louise, is that opportunities like this do happen occasionally, and anytime you can one-up the casino, jump on it!

DEAR MARK: *When a pit boss brought in new cards on our blackjack game, a friend I'm with tells me to lower my bet on the first shuffle. Does it really make any difference?* **John D.**

Whether I answer yes or no, John, it's still bound to stir an argument among purists on both sides of the issue.

First, a study I recently read stated that a new deck of cards only becomes random after it's been shuffled seven times. It's also my experience that most casinos only require a dealer to shuffle, even with a new deck on the game, from three to five times. So why are these statements important? Because, when a new deck of cards arrives on your game fresh out of the box, it comes in a predefined order (A-K hearts, A-K clubs, K-A diamonds, K-A spades), which contains 10-value card clumps not completely broken up by the initial shuffle.

So though my answer leans towards yes, albeit mildly, I do confess I also back off until the second shuffle—which should make the cards as random as they can be.

DEAR MARK: *What are those funny little blackjack abbreviations like H17, RSA and DOA mean that I've seen on casino newspaper advertising or internet gambling forums?* **Bud T.**

Authors Ovid Demaris and Ed Reid's conception of DOA was the cautionary advice they gave in their 1963 book, *The Truth About Las Vegas.* "The surest way to beat Las Vegas is to get off the plane that has taken you there and walk straight into the propeller." It's actually the rule variations/conditions that each particular casino offers for blackjack. Below are some you would typically see.

BSE = Basic Strategy Edge
H17 = Hit soft 17 (dealer must hit)
S17 = Stand on any 17 (dealer must stand)
DOA = Double On Any first two cards
D10 = Double on 10 or 11 only
DAS = Double After Splitting is allowed
RSA = Re-Splitting Aces is allowed
ESR = Early Surrender
LSR = Late Surrender
O/U = Over/Under 13 side bets are allowed

DEAR MARK: *In some of your columns you mention the word "grind." What do you mean by that?* **Ray R.**

In the language of casino gambling, Ray, *grind* can be used in a variety of ways. A *grind player* is generally a term associated with a low roller. A *grind joint* is a casino that caters to these low rollers. Then there's the grind down. This is where the casino eventually wins all the player's money due to the built-in advantage it has on all wagers. Finally, the *grind system.* This is any system used by a player that attempts to win small amounts frequently against the casino. Unfortunately, the latter is highly unlikely.

"There will eventually be a half dozen properties in Las Vegas that will command 90 percent of the public attention, and every other property will be a dormitory"
– ALEX YEMENIDJIAN PRESIDENT, MGM GRAND INC.

♠ 42 ♠
Fiscal Ruin Possible When You Select the Wrong Machine

DEAR MARK: *Well, now that you've got me "Hooked on Winning" (I bought your tapes, good stuff), I have a follow-up observation and a question. I took a well-deserved day off from work yesterday and hit the two Indian casinos here in Connecticut (Foxwoods and Mohegan Sun). My goal was to restrict myself exclusively to video poker. First, you are right on the money in your observation that you have to LOOK for a 9/6 machine, at least in the 25¢ and 50¢ denominations. I found a 25¢ 9/6 machine "buried" in a bank of machines at the Mohegan Sun and had real good luck with it. I encountered my first 8/5 progressive machine at Foxwoods, but I was surprised to see it was NOT a jacks-or-better machine. Rather, it was a two pair or better machine. So instead of having a payoff with just a high pair, a player needed two pairs to get a return. Is this typical of an 8/5 progressive machine or would you say this is player adverse?* **Mike K.**

Take copious notes here, Mike. Two words describe the above-mentioned machine at Foxwoods—RIP OFF.

It is called an 8/5-video poker machine because of the 8-for-1 payoff for a full house and 5-for-1 payoff for a flush. Getting paid for a high pair (jacks-or-better) is an absolute necessity when playing video poker.

On a traditional jacks-or-better machine you will hit a high pair, two pair and three of a kind at a rate of 41%. Expect no return 55% of the time. As for just the high pair, its relative frequency occurs every 4.75 hands, or 21.053% of the time. Why, Mike, give the casino an additional 21%?

You need the jacks-or-better to keep you in the game. Needing two pair for a return is giving the casino a license to steal from the non-informed player.

DEAR MARK: *I am making my annual pilgrimage to Las Vegas next month. On my last two trips I believe I have paid exorbitant room rates—$89 a night. Both times the casino hotel wouldn't bargain on these high prices. I prefer not to get stung for a room, figuring they are going to get my money at the tables anyway. Any suggestions?* **Stephanie G.**

I have booked at least a dozen trips to Lost Wages with Las Vegas Reservation Systems. Their toll free number is 1-800-222-0892. Las Vegas Reservation Systems guarantees the lowest prices at all the hotels, plus they offer air packages and car rentals. You can even book online at their internet web site (www.lvrs.com). As for Las Vegas Reservation Systems being the absolute cheapest, I can't say for sure, as I haven't verified their guarantee. I can state that over the past two years I've never paid more that $39 for a room, which is well below the rack rate.

DEAR MARK: *In years past, Atlantic City casinos used to invited my play with not only a free bus ride to the Shore but a bucket worth of coins to get me started. Seems lately the casinos are getting tighter and tighter with their customers. Are they?* **Marty S.**

Yes, Marty, what you perceive is correct my friend. Those rolls of nickels to induce initial play are evaporating as the amount of money the casinos give bus customers spirals downward. Today, AC casinos pay an average of $16.54 to customers bussed in from outer markets, down from the low $20s last year.

It could be worse, Marty. When you have the only game in town like Casino Windsor in Canada, duping $40 out of patrons for valet parking seems appropriate to casino management. Or how about a sole riverboat casino that monopolizes a market? You not only get squat but charged to grace their gambling joint.

So granted, Marty, though you're $4 lighter in the bucket, you still have to love a casino that pays you to play.

♠ 43 ♠
Player May Not Merit a Frolic Frenzy

DEAR MARK: *When I stayed at the NY, NY Hotel and Casino (Vegas), I played BJ and whenever I wanted a comp for food or anything, they said just put it on your room charge and your play will be evaluated. Well, that was my first and last time. When I checked out they didn't comp my food or beverage, only the room. What gives?* **Scott R.**

Your question, Scott, was not specific as to how much you were betting or how long you were playing blackjack. That makes a huge difference when it comes to the casino doling out the goodies.

Casino comps are generally figured in the following manner. The pit boss (bull) will take your average bet multiplied by hours played, speed of the game and the casino advantage of that game. The final figure, in theory, should equal your loss. Comps are then rewarded accordingly. Conning the casino to give you more comps than your play deserves is nearly impossible now that corporate America is minding the store.

As for your room, it was easy to comp because it is a controlled price. It can take as little as $20 to dress out a room for the evening. When it comes to food and drink, many players charge the feedbox huge, hit the wine list hard and drive the comp expenditure to a point no pit boss could justify. You very well could have been a typical blackjack player playing $10 a hand, 50 hands an hour. Risking $500 and losing two percent of that is a total loss of $10 to the house for every 60 minutes of play. Hardly worth carte blanc treatment by the casino. But one complimentary buffet, possibly a room? Yes, you probably qualify.

You could, Scott, increase your prominence in the casino's eyes by playing $100 a hand for eight hours, but is it really worth blowing a king's ransom just to get a shot at the steak and lobster house and a few bottles of bubbly? That would be dumb, foolish and costly if you can't afford to wager $100 a hand.

DEAR MARK: *My friends and I get together once a month for a night of poker. We were playing seven card, high low split. All the cards had been dealt and the betting started. Brant opened and checked. There were a couple of bets around the table and then it came back to Brant. He saw the bets and raised. At that time I protested and explained to him that because he had checked he couldn't raise. I didn't get much support at the table for this claim. I thought it was common knowledge. What's the ruling?* **Woody J.**

The decision from Nevada: you lose. All the Nevada poker rooms play check and raise. But because Nevada is not your kitchen table, house rules like check and raise among belching buddies, should be discussed at the onset of the evening. Not after an argument ensues.

DEAR MARK: *I have heard that Atlantic City casinos allow card counters but Nevada casinos do not. True?* **Jimmy C.**

True, Jimmy, but a minefield of obstacles still hinders card counters on the Jersey shore. On September 15, 1982 the Appellate Division of the New Jersey Superior Court ruled that a player could not be discriminated against because of his playing skills (counting). In Nevada, laws allow casinos to operate as private clubs and you can be legally ejected for using your intellect. Brains need to be checked at the door.

Atlantic City casinos still have an assortment of countermeasures to offset a counter's advantage. They lawfully impede skilled blackjack players by using eight-deck shoes, shuffle at will to thwart bet variance and instruct the dealers to move the cut card near the top of the shoe on suspected counters.

The alien was reporting back to the Supreme Master of his spaceship following a visit to earth. "I visited a gathering of female earthlings in what is clearly some sort of shrine. They all sit quietly in rows in a large hall. Each earthling has a number of small cards in front of her. A male earthling sits on an elevated platform constantly calling out numbers to which the earthlings listen with rapt attention. At the height of the ceremony the male utters a number which obviously has a religious significance. At this point one female shouts at the top of her voice the utterance 'BINGO,' and the rest of the assembled multitude reply, 'DAMN IT."

♣ 44 ♠
Is it Gaming or Gambling?

DEAR MARK: *On a regular basis you refer to casino entertainment as gambling. The industry refers to it as gaming. Who's right?* **Steven S.**

Depends on the prejudiced authority. My bias, Steven, is that of an irreverent syndicated gambling columnist and player advocate—hence, it's gambling. My dear friends who still work in the gambling industry in upper-management have an intoxicated partiality toward gaming.

But this juicy morsel crossed my desk compliments of Bob G., a reader of the *Traverse City Record-Eagle*. Bob sent me an Associated Press article written about the literary folks at Lake Superior State University. The school has an annual list of misused, overused and useless words and phrases it wants to banish from the English language. Lake Superior releases this list each Jan. 1 after gathering thousands of submissions nominated from academia, business, journalism, politics, the military and sports. On their 22nd annual list is gaming. Comments: **Gaming**. Used to seduce people into thinking they're not really gambling.

DEAR MARK: *As a stockbroker I should know better. That is, when to get out of a bad trade, or in the case of gambling, bet. But when it comes to casino gambling, I tend to stay far too long for my own good. This tends to lead to losses much greater than if I left earlier with a small gain. How common an occurrence is this in a casino?* **Jeff G.**

Jeff, you play in the world casino, Wall Street; doesn't your industry have an aphorism, "Be a bull or a bear, but never a hog?" Like many, many other players, Jeff, you exhibit signs of poor money management. And money management, my friend, is really nothing more than character management. To truly become a winning player you have to first know when to get up and walk.

87

DEAR MARK: *What does the term "horn" bet mean in craps?* **Clayburn P.**

A "horn" bet is a one-roll proposition wager which is a combination of any craps (2, 3, 12) and a bet on the 11. It pays off according to the individual payoff for each number, less the three chips that were lost. Do I recommend said wager? NO. Craps offers two kinds of one-roll bets—hopeless and wretched. Although proposition bets have seemingly lofty payoffs, the house edge is way to high too waste your hard-earned money on them.

DEAR MARK: *Recently in Puerto Rico, a player at the baccarat table kept calling out "monkey" as the player who was dealing out the cards was about to draw one from the shoe. What did this mean?* **Pat Z.**

In gamb-lingo, I've heard the term monkey used two ways. 1. A sucker. 2. A face card.

My guess is that our articulated friend was hoping the next card out of the shoe would be a face card so his hand would win out. Example: Our wishful bettor has wagered the "bank" hand and is sitting pretty with a two-card 7. The "player" hand total is a 3, subsequently needing a hit. A "monkey" would not improve the "player" hand as face cards and 10s have zero card value in baccarat. The "bank" hand would prevail.

DEAR MARK: *What is the worst bet to make on a crap game?* **Kevin K.**

The worst wager on a crap game, or any table game for that matter, is the "any seven" bet on the dice table. This one-roll proposition bet has a house edge of 16.7%.

"Gambling: The sure way of getting nothing from something."
– WILSON MIZNER

♠ 45 ♠
Heed the Golden Rule of Gambling

DEAR MARK: *If there was one golden rule of gambling you would give to first-time players, what would it be?* **Bob H.**

The same golden rule that Peter Lynch, the legendary stock picker and former fund manager of Fidelity Magellan, believes; "Never invest money you can't afford to lose." The same holds true in gambling. Never gamble above your means or with money you can't afford to lose.

DEAR MARK: *I have read that you should always play the maximum amount of coins when playing the slot machines. I have a friend who argues that you will hit jackpots more often if you play only one coin at a time, then bet more. In the long run, does it make any difference at all how many coins I play at a time?* **Clyde B.**

The idea behind your friend's theory is that you will save money "priming" the machine for a big jackpot. Till I'm blue in the face, this won't happen. All pulls are random, Clyde, and the number of coins played has absolutely no effect on determining when or what type of winning symbols will appear on the machine.

For almost all multiple-pay and multiple-play machines, the maximum coin line tends to yield a better percentage payback. Note on the paytable the proportional difference in the size of your payoff. Example: One coin inserted pays 500 coins, two coins; 1000 coins, three coins; 4000 returned. Paydirt when three coins are played.

If you can afford to play the maximum coin amount, do so. If you cannot, switch to a lower denomination machine.

DEAR MARK: *Recently I was on a blackjack game minding my own business and as you say "playing with my hard-earned money," when out of the blue an individual standing behind me (he wasn't playing, just watching) decided he would instruct me on how to play each and every hand. How would you have handled this annoyance?* **Ronnie G.**

The patron you described is called a kibitzer: A spectator at a game who makes unsolicited comments, unwanted advice and drives everyone bonkers. Solution: Call over the pit boss and explain your predicament. He or she will have a very sympathetic ear since the nuisance is not gambling.

DEAR MARK: *Over the years I have been an avid keno player. Now after reading your comments many times about keno, I have refrained from playing and limit my play to the many other games and bets you recommend. Coincidentally, I seem to be winning more. Though I have never hit a keno ticket solid, my favorite tickets in the past were a 5-spot, 7-spot, 8-spot and a 9-spot. What were the odds of me hitting one of those tickets?* **Alice C.**

In past articles, Alice, I have listed the astronomical odds of some keno tickets that need calculators using exponential notations to figure. Below I'll list the probability of hitting the smaller tickets solid.

1/1	One in 4
2/2	One in 16
3/3	One in 72
4/4	One in 326
5/5	One in 1,550
6/6	One in 7,752
7/7	One in 40,979
8/8	One in 230,114
9/9	One in 1,380,687
10/10	One in 8,911,711

And what will the average casino pay you for hitting a solid 10? A $2 wager returns a measly $45,000 in Atlantic City and $100,000 in Nevada. Chump change considering your chances are almost nine million to one. Doesn't the lottery start to sound good about now?

♠ 46 ♠
Analogies of Greed and Pomposity

DEAR MARK: *On my last six trips to Gulfport, MS, I've come home a winner playing slots. I believe it's beyond luck now. I just have this certain feeling when to play a particular machine. I've been so successful lately that I feel I should go to dollar machines, or higher, versus the quarter ones and win even more money. Am I on to something here?* **Jon S.**

Jon, may I share two stories with you? One deals with arrogance and the other with the incessant craving for more.

An old Polish folk tale tells of a fisherman who lives in a hovel by the sea and catches a magical fish that grants his humble desire for a cabin and enough to eat. After a week, he is no longer satisfied and demands larger quarters, and once again the fish grants him his wish. The sequence of catch and release repeats itself for six weeks until the fisherman lives in a castle, then demands the finest palace. For his insolence, the fish casts him back to the hovel by the sea.

For the second story, let's stick with the water theme. "God himself cannot sink this ship." Those were the quotes throughout the newspapers prior to the Titanic making her first passage across the big pond. She was appropriately named, as Titans always dared to challenge the gods, and for their arrogance they were cast down into hell.

At best, Jon, by challenging the gaming gods absorbed in your spirit of rapacity, you're on the Atlantic ocean in a one-man lifeboat with a slow leak. And the sound I hear? Pssssssss.

91

DEAR MARK: *I very much enjoy the historical questions you answer. Where do you find the answers to the most obscure questions? Also, how about trying mine? Tell me about the history of keno in this country.* **Sylvia R.**

Around 200 B.C. in China, Cheung Leung introduced the lottery, the forerunner to modern day keno, to fund his army. Because of its overwhelming success, it continued, and additional proceeds from future lotteries were used to fund major projects such as the Great Wall.

In the 1860s when the building of the railroads in the United States offered promise to Chinese immigrants, they brought a game, the Chinese lottery, to America. As the game's popularity grew, it evolved from a 120-grid ticket used in the railroad camps to an 80-number ticket called Keno.

You wanted to know my sources, Sylvia. This sweetmeat of enlightenment came from the placemats at the coffee shop at Karl's Silver Nugget in Sparks, Nevada. Found above the placemats were cheap, terrific breakfast specials—and for some readers, that's more valuable information than the Keno answer.

DEAR MARK: *Don't you think that when you write about long-shot slot machines like Megabucks, you induce play rather than helping a player refrain from playing?* **Stanley F.**

The goal of this column is not to shill for the casinos but to inform players on the exact cost of an evening's entertainment. I am of the opinion, Stanley, that players should know exactly what their chances are of hitting the big jackpots. Some casinos do post the paybacks on their machines, but not the true odds of hitting a jackpot. If they posted the odds, no one in his right mind would play those machines. You will note, that I continually write that your chances are slim to none for a life of opulence when playing Megabucks.

Unfortunately, no amount of education from me, nor the casino disclosing the enormous odds right on a machine, will curb a player's appetite for hitting it rich. Every slot participant believes he or she will be the exception to the rule; she will beat the celestial gods; it is he who will come home a victorious contestant against ABC casino.

And every so often, Stanley, to induce a Pavlov saliva reaction, you will read in the paper that Mabel, from Ames, Iowa, hit it big, real big.

♠ 47 ♠
Guerrilla Gambling 101

DEAR MARK: *Casinos must make loads of money off constant losers like myself. Anything I can do to stop the flow of money always going in one direction?* **Sandra R.**

But do you have a smile on your face when you lose, Sandra? I ask that because Bob Stupak, a major casino operator in Las Vegas, was quoted in *U.S. News and World Report* saying; "It's our duty to extract as much money from the customer as we can and send them home with a smile on their face."

Believe me, Sandra, casinos are a green felt jungle and you're playing war. But that doesn't mean the casinos win every battle. You can fight back by becoming a Guerrilla Gambler. How? By only making bets that have a 2% house advantage or less. When you do, you'll stand a good chance of turning the tables in your favor, staying in action longer, having fun and, yes, stopping the flow of your hard-earned cash going to the opposite forces (casino corporate headquarters).

Here are some of my favorite guerrilla warfare wagers. All have less than a 2% house advantage and can be found in most casinos coast to coast.

Blackjack: A game that many play, but few play well. Solution: Playing perfect basic strategy. Perfect basic strategy will bring the house advantage down to well under 1%.

Craps: Want three outstanding craps wagers? The pass and come line bets, preceding wagers with odds, and placing the 6 or 8. All have a house advantage of 1.5% or lower. Stay away from those proposition bets (hardways, field bets, one number rolls, etc.) entirely. Some can have a house advantage as high as 16%.

93

Baccarat: Baccarat definitely evokes images of Monte Carlo and James Bond, but don't let the mystique of the game intimidate you. It's one of the easiest casino games to play (you don't even have to know the rules because correct hitting is predetermined), and the stakes are relatively low when you play on a mini-baccarat table. The house advantage is either 1.17% when betting the bank hand or 1.36% with a player hand wager. Skip the tie bet: House advantage 14%.

Video Poker: There is no such thing as a bad video poker machine, only bad pay tables. Here's another opportunity where playing perfect basic strategy on a machine with a decent pay schedule can reduce the house advantage to well under 1%.

Slots: Yes, you're reading it right, SLOTS. But only "liberal" slot machines. What I mean by liberal slots are those in casinos that advertise a higher payback percentage—like a 98.5% return—on selected machines. Be forewarned, these high payback slots are usually only found where casino competition is fierce; plus when you do find a casino advertising liberal paybacks, you'll then need to ask someone in slot personnel which machines those are. Yes there is some skill involved besides pulling a handle when playing slots—it's machine selection.

As you can see, Sandra, all through the casino you'll find decent wagers. Some, like blackjack or video poker, involve skill, while with others, it's placing the correct bet in the right place on the layout. But identifying the guerrilla wagers was just step one, Sandra. Next you must acquire a good solid education for your favorite game. Then you're truly on your way to becoming a Guerrilla Gambler.

Now repeat this phrase after me: "The smarter I play, the luckier I'll be."

DEAR MARK: *In past columns you have stated "unequivocally" to avoid long-shot keno tickets. How about the simple three-spot ticket?* **Kay B.**

There is only one bigger waste of money than playing any keno ticket, Kay. That's playing two!

♠ 48 ♠
You No Longer Need to Cut Off Both Ends of the Ham

DEAR MARK: *I learned craps from my father, who learned it from his dad. We play your recommended pass line bet along with continual betting on the seven to hedge our line bet. In past columns you don't agree with that logic. Please explain.* **Marvin B.**

Marvin, before you advance your crapology advice to future generations, may I share an anecdotal tale with you?

One day a young girl watched her mother prepare a ham for Thanks
-giving dinner.
"Mom, why did you cut off both ends of the ham?" the daughter asked.
"Because my mother always did," said the mother.
"But why?"
"I don't know—why don't you call Granny and find out why."
So the daughter called Granny and asked her. "Granny, when you prepared your hams for baking, why did you always cut off both ends?"
"My mother always did it," said Granny.
"But why?"
"I don't know—why don't you call your Great-grandmother and ask her?" So the daughter preceded to telephone Great-grandmother to inquire why traditionally her family always cut off both ends of a ham before cooking it.
"Great-grandma, when you prepared your ham for baking, you al ways cut off both ends—why?"
"Well," Great-grandma said, "the pan was too small."

It is time, Marvin, to let go of your genealogically inspired gambling theories. Though you feel you are hedging you wager by betting the seven, it still doesn't change the house advantage of 16.7%. By sticking strictly to a pass line wager, maybe, just maybe, you will be the first in your clan to win some real money at craps.

DEAR MARK: *Does it make sense keeping a kicker in video poker?* **Marty M.**

NEVER, repeat never, hold a kicker. Holding kickers (K, K, A) to any pair reduces your return by more than 5%.

DEAR MARK: *I like to bet the don't side on a crap game. Isn't it a slightly better wager than a pass line bet?* **Kenny K.**

You are correct in assuming, Kenny, that the don't pass bet (seven rolling before the point) is a marginally better wager—a 1.4 percent casino advantage versus the pass line's 1.41 percent—but craps is a game of community esprit, everyone in it for the win together. By betting the opposite you become the adversary, a villain against the majority of players.

Why let the casino off the hook?

DEAR MARK: *What was the largest amount ever won in roulette?* **Jason C.**

In January, 1994, a computer programmer from London, England, wagered $220,000 on a single spin at the Horseshoe Club in Las Vegas. Placing the whole amount on red, he watched as the ball found the red 7. Picking up his one-roll winnings, he quickly deposited $440,000 in the cashier's cage. The tuxedo-clad gentleman was knowledgeable enough to play on the Horseshoe's single zero roulette table, cutting the house edge from 5.26 to 2.7%.

DEAR MARK: *I really enjoy keno. Would you recommend video keno or a live-action game?* **Rosa M.**

The correct answer, Rosa, would be to suggest politely neither.

The medium house advantage on all live keno games is approximately 28%. On a video keno game it is 7.5%. Why lower? Video keno has better paytables. Take the 8-spot ticket: By hitting four of eight on a video keno machine, you double your money. You'll never find that on a live keno game.

On paper, it looks like video poker is the better deal. Not so fast my friend. At $1 a pop, the most you could lose on a live game is about $15, as that is the average number of games called per hour. A typical video keno player can burn through $15 in quarters in under five minutes.

I recommend, Rosa, for those with a keno fixation, video poker instead.

♠ 49 ♠
So What's All the Hoopla Over Megabucks

DEAR MARK: *Recently Megabucks surpassed the current record of more than $11 million dollars. A few questions please. First, is there an easy way to find out the current progressive amount without going to a casino? Second, do you get paid half up front and the remainder over the next 10 years? Finally, when it approaches record levels, should I join the excitement and run out and play?* **Lois H.**

Lois, I have never quite understood the frenzy when the Nevada Megabucks jackpot rises to a level where some fortunate soul rewrites the slot jackpot record book. Granted, it is a new milestone for IGT's MegaJackpot systems, but most players don't realize that Megabucks is a tougher beat than most state lotteries. Additionally, you also have to buck up three dollars (3-coin bet) versus your one dollar donation to state education. And what are the true odds of hitting a Megabucks bonanza? 16,777,216 to one.

For those in the dark, Megabucks is an IGT (NYSE: IGT) MegaJackpot slot system that connects 747 machines in 136 Nevada casinos to a primary jackpot that builds from a base amount of $5 million. Now I don't care which state you live in, but I will wager dollars to donuts that all state lotteries have had more winners and given away more money than IGT's Megabucks. So what's the big deal? No hidden camera investigation here, just PR department without peer that hypes the hysteria.

You also asked, Lois, about following current jackpot totals. All IGT Nevada MegaJackpot systems totals are available by calling tollfree 888-448-2WIN (888-448-2946).

Finally, Lois, Megabuck winners do not receive a chunk of change up front; instead, International Game Technology, the Reno-based slot machine maker that created and operates Megabucks, pays the winner in 25 annual installments.

DEAR MARK: *What is the specific house edge when taking odds on a crap game?* **Tom S.**

Here are the percentages in favor of the house for pass line and come bettors when you take full advantage of various odds bets.

Pass line (Come) no odds	1.41%
Single odds	0.85%
Double odds	0.61%
Triple odds	0.47%
Five times odds	0.32%
10 times odds	0.18%

Minus being a sophisticated card counter, taking odds on a pass line bet is the absolute "best bet" in the house. The odds themselves have a casino advantage of zero. A highly recommended wager.

DEAR MARK: *What is a "Duke" in craps?* **Leo S.**

A "Duke" is a monster hand on a crap game, which all but casino owners wish would go on until the end of time. "He shot the dice forever in the name of John Wayne," a dealer would say after a lengthy roll concludes.

Those of us fortunate to work the south end of Lake Tahoe know a "Duke" as employee Steve Ditchkus, who worked at Bill's Casino. Unfortunately, our loss is someone else's (players, fellow employee's) gain, since he's moved on to work for Harrah's in Topeka, Kansas.

I wish I had 2,000 words just to share the fun times we've all had working, playing, gambling, etc. with Steve, but suffice it to say that if someone were to write a book on gambling at Lake Tahoe and didn't mention "the Duke," they wouldn't have done their research.

DEAR MARK: *Do the casinos really care if you win?* **Jake M.**

Win or lose, it makes no difference to the Lord's of Chance—just as long as you're a player. Preferably a loyal returning player willing and able to give it all back.

♠ 50 ♠
I Play Occasionally, Twice a Week

DEAR MARK: *I've got a dinner riding on this. My husband believes that you, being conservative when it comes to casino gambling, would never play the lottery. Do you?* **Rachel P.**

I once asked a friend of mine if he ever played the lotto and he fired back, "I play occasionally, twice a week." Slightly different than my personal approach, mainly because I come from a background of evaluating odds in every playing situation. So yes, I'll come clean and confess I play, but only when the jackpot is close to the true odds of hitting a (California) 6/51 ticket—which happens to be one in 18,009,460.

Now as for lotto strategy, I just play quick-pick numbers. Quick-picks provide a more random spread of numbers coupled with the fact that the pot isn't divided up as much as when you play birthday or sequence numbers. Obviously this will result in a much larger payoff if you win.

Here's what I mean, Rachel. One of the most popular number combinations in every state lottery is 1-2-3-4-5-6. Illustrating this, I'll use the September, 1990, Florida $106 million jackpot as an example. Won by six players, the jackpot netted the chosen few $17 million apiece. Sure, we'll all take that without complaining, but for that same jackpot, more than 52,000 people played the numbers 1-2-3-4-5-6. See how playing a sequence combination of numbers will affect the payoffs to eventual winners? The same can be said with those lucky birthday dates as well. Over 65% of the numbers played in most state lotteries are under 31.

So, Rachel, you win the dinner, and that's how I play. Close to true odds, and random numbers.

DEAR MARK: *One thing I like about the casino I play in is the way they handle coins. They don't. You insert bills and play on credits only. When you cash out, the machine prints a ticket and you take it to the cashier's cage (within 2 hours). It really is cleaner. Do you agree?* **Donny M.**

Donny, you didn't mention the casino by name, but I suspect it's on an Indian Reservation because many operate using this method of coin exchange—for which I firmly give two thumbs down! Why? Because you become prisoner to one machine—which has a huge built-in mathematical edge—putting the casino in position to grind the $20 right out of you.

Let's get realistic here. Who really has the discipline to get up from that cushy seat, walk over to the cashier's cage, turn in the credit slip for cash, and then find another suitable machine? Far too many undisciplined players just won't free themselves from this ball and chain scenario and, unfortunately, will play their credits down to nothing. So $20 inserted most likely becomes $20 for the casino.

DEAR MARK: *What is the difference between a soft comp and a hard comp?* **Leta R.**

Before you try strong-arming a casino to get your fair share of comps, it behooves you to know the difference between a hard comp and a soft comp. One is much easier to get from the casino than the other.

Hard comps are reimbursements for airline tickets, golf, concerts, off-site casino shows or anything else that would cost the casino real out-of-pocket dollars. Soft comps are cocktails, restaurant expenses and shows that the casinos produce themselves. Whales (high limit players) can get anything their hearts desire, but if you're a low-limit player, go for a soft comp because casinos technically purchase them wholesale and bill them to a comp account retail.

Lottery: A tax on people who are bad at math.
    – SPOTTED ON A BUMPER IN NEVADA

♠ 51 ♠
The Language of Craps

DEAR MARK: *I tried playing craps for the first time on a recent trip to Las Vegas. I stuck with the bets you mention on your tapes and actually walked away from the crap table $200 ahead. And though I was up $200, I still found the game intimidating. Mostly because I couldn't understand what numbers the dealer was calling. No wonder it scares so many players away. So just what number is "Little Joe from Kokomo?"* **Ralph S.**

Your question, Ralph, is the reason why more than 90 percent who visit casinos deny themselves playing what many consider the most engaging, exhilarating game the casino has to offer. Not only that, if craps is played correctly, the percentage favoring the house is less than video poker, slots, roulette and even blackjack; that is, Ralph, if players like you follow the fundamental principles I've laid out on my audio tapes and stick to pass line bets with odds or placing the six and eight.

But still, when the game gets electric, the communal consciousness of the players leads to a table of whooping, rooting and apprehensive participants. This creates a game that both confuses and overwhelms. Now add your complaint: A dealer (stickman) with a rattan rake in hand moving the game pace along at high speeds, yelling calls that only someone in the industry might understand. Your best bet is to learn the lingo.

By no means, Ralph, is the language eloquent, but it is expressive and the best way to learn is by putting the dice in your hands. So shooter, you're coming out, hands up, feet off the table, let'em loose and I'll make the calls.

101

TWO: "Craps," "two aces," "rats eyes," "snake eyes," "push the don't," "eleven in a shoe store," "twice in the rice," "two craps two, two bad boys from Illinois."

THREE: "Craps," "ace-deuce," "ace caught a deuce," "winner on the dark side," "three craps three, the indicator," "small ace deuce, can't produce," "the other side of eleven's tummy." (Here's an example of an old-time crap dealer, Judd, who invents a call that made its way across Nevada to a carpet joint that I've worked in. It doesn't make sense, like many of the calls, so your confusion is fitting.)

FOUR: "Little Joe," "little Joe from Kokomo," "hit us in the tu tu," "ace trey, the country way."

FIVE: "After five, the field's alive," "thirty-two juice roll" (OJ's jersey number), "little Phoebe," "fiver, fiver, racetrack driver," "we got the fever."

SIX: "Big Red, catch'em in the corner," "like a blue chip stock," "pair-o-treys, waiter's roll," "the national average," "sixie from Dixie."

SEVEN: "Seven out, line away," "grab the money," "five two, you're all through," "six ace, end of the race," "front line winner, back line skinner," "six one, you're all done," "seven's a bruiser, the front line's a loser," "up pops the devil," "Benny Blue, you're all through."

EIGHT: "A square pair, like mom and dad," "Ozzie and Harriet," "the windows," "eighter from Decatur."

NINE: "Center field," "center of the garden," "ocean liner niner," "Nina from Pasadena," "What shot Jesse James? A forty-five."

TEN: "Puppy paws," "pair-a-roses," "pair of sunflowers," "the big one on the end."

ELEVEN: "Yo leven," "yo levine the dancing queen," "six five, no jive."

TWELVE: "Craps," "boxcars," "atomic craps," "all the spots we got," "outstanding in your field," "triple dipple, in the lucky ducky," "double saw on boxcars."

Look there, Ralph, you just rolled a seven. Column's over. Cinco dos, adios.

♠ 52 ♠
The Legacy of The Gambler

DEAR MARK: *Were you surprised when the Navajo Indians recently voted against casino gambling on their reservation? I thought that every tribe wants casino gaming. Why didn't the Navajos jump on the wagon train (pardon the pun).* **Brady M.**

If you believe in the Navajo legend, of The Gambler, you would know that gambling has a deep cultural resonance for the Navajo. Their oral tradition has many stories warning against the dangers of overindulging in gambling. Also, tribal president Albert Hales opposed the measure because federal law requires the Navajos to negotiate a casino agreement with the states. Hale believes that such an agreement erodes the tribe's status as a sovereign nation. Plus, the tribe voted against casino gambling on their reservation just three years ago. So, Brady, for the above reasons, particularly the traditional myth of an out-of-control gambler who goes out and wins—and then loses—everything, I was not surprised by the Navajo's rejection of casino gambling.

As legend has it, the tale begins when the Spirit of the Sun, a gambler himself, wants a large piece of turquoise held by a Pueblo tribe. The sun sends his son, The Gambler, to Earth to wager for the invaluable sea-green stone. The Gambler is unbeatable.

He wins the rain, snow, plants and flowers, and everything else in sight, leaving the tribe impoverished. Eventually The Gambler wins the turquoise but wants to gamble against his father for it. So the Spirit of the Sun teaches his other offspring how to gamble and win the turquoise back from his brother. The second son is victorious and ultimately he shoots The Gambler into the sky with his large bow.

So, Brady, you decide. Was it being at the states' mercy, a rebuff three years earlier, or folklore that tells its people to be very cautious when it comes to gambling? Myself, I believe in ni'hwiilbiihi, "the one that wins the people."

103

DEAR MARK: *I got into a beef with a pit boss over picking up my pass line bet after the point was made. Can a pass line bet be taken off the table once a point has been established?* **Don D.**

A pass line bet is a contract wager committing your participation until an eventual outcome. Sorry, Don; it lays, it plays.

DEAR MARK: *In past columns, you've stated the benefits of playing slots that advertise returns of 98.5% versus machines that pay back 93%. Come on, Mark, we're talking just a few dollars difference. What's the big deal?* **Noreen D.**

The "big deal" is that the casino knows the average Joe and Josephine don't play through their money just once but keeps playing their tray (credit) return over and over again during the course of their stay. That's why finding higher payback machines is so important. Example: On a 93% return machine if you were to play your entire $100, you can expect back, "in theory," $93. Of course, the casino anticipates your playing the $93, so expect a return of $86. Put in the $86, and your return will be $80. Play through the $80, get back, $74. Can you see, Noreen, how the casino is grinding away at your crispy Ben Franklin?

Now, using the same example on a machine returning 98.5%, put in $100 and get back $98.50. Play that, and you'll get $97 back. Put in the $97, expect a return of $95. Of course this is all based on a pre-programmed computer chip in the slot, but see how much better it is to play the higher payback machines? It keeps you in action much longer, long enough possibly to hit a decent jackpot.

"Remember this: The house doesn't beat the player. It just gives him the opportunity to beat himself."
—NICHOLAS (NICK THE GREEK) DANDALOS

♠ 53 ♠
Bad Checks, Loaded Dice and Coin Flips

DEAR MARK: *Trick question. If a friend and I flip a coin in the air and bet on its result, would the coin be considered an unlawful gambling device?* **Josh L.**

A coin itself is not a gambling device *per se* because it was created and designed for a specific purpose. However, the coin becomes an illegal apparatus, subject to forfeiture by the state, when it is flipped in the air and wagers are made on its eventual outcome.

DEAR MARK: *How does a pitboss on a crap game identify loaded dice?* **Donald M.**

Called the "Spin" or "Pivot" test, a boxman on a crap game will hold the dice loosely between his thumb and forefinger at diagonally opposite corners and gently spin the dice. A fair cube will spin smoothly and its revolution will stop in a natural way. A loaded die, because of the extra weight, will pivot back in a distinguished manner at the end of its rotation.

At home, you can test for loaded dice by filling a tall glass with water and dropping the cubes in gently. Repeat this action several times with a different number on top. If the same number appears repeatedly, they're loaded. Why? Because the weighted dice will turn toward the bottom as they fall each time.

DEAR MARK: *While at a party for the final game of the World Series, I bet an acquaintance, not friend, $300 on the game. He took Cleveland, lost, and paid me with a personal check. Yes, the check bounced. Do I have any legal recourse against him?* **Billy C.**

Sorry, Billy. Unless you own a casino, accepting a check to cover a gambling debt is not collectable in a court of law, even if you made the bet in Nevada where sports betting is legal.

DEAR MARK: *What do you think of all the new games that keep popping up on the casino floor?* **Lyle O.**

This past week I noticed yet another new game, 21 Stud, that offers a bonus jackpot for a naturally dealt, no draw royal flush. Casinos get goo-goo-ga-ga about introducing any game that will induce additional play. Their marketing department goes head over heels highlighting the fact that if you get a natural royal flush, you will be paid 1,000 to one. What they forget to tell you, this column continually will. The chances of getting a naturally dealt, no draw royal flush are 659,740 to one.

For a new game to survive in today's tough gaming market, table games must have some sort of progressive or jackpot to generate play. Unfortunately, the odds are usually long and tall against the customer. Be an educated player, Lyle. On all these new games and side bonus bets, you might as well pass.

DEAR MARK: *How come some slot machines advertise a relatively high payout but still send you home devoid of casino loot?* **Pearl R.**

Pearl, the answer, in one word, is what makes every casino owner's pockets bulge with your cash—CHURN. That higher payout rate only applies if you don't continue to bet your winning credits. Unfortunately, that's not the way most people play. They recycle (churn) their money back through the cybernetic one-armed bandit.

Casino operators have long realized the advantage they have between an advertised payout and the coinage they eventually reap. How so you ask? By comparing credits won versus credits paid out. Player behavior is such that credits won are generally replayed, and replayed and replayed again, resulting mathematically in a much greater chance of eventually tapping out. They may advertise a 95 percent return, but after the churn takes place, you'll generally go home lighter in the wallet.

"Life is a gamble at terrible odds.
If it was a bet, you wouldn't take it."
– TOM STOPPARD ROSENCRANTZ AND GUILDENSTERN ARE DEAD

♠ 54 ♠
Craps Wagers that put You in Lollipop Land

DEAR MARK: *On numerous occasions you recommend only pass line bets with odds and placing the six or eight on the crap table. How about listing the worst bets in craps so us rookies can stop playing them?* **Larry J.**

Below are the list of sucker bets found on a crap game along with their house edge.

Big 6 & 8	(9.1%)
Hardway 6 or 8	(9.1%)
Hardway 4 or 10	(11.1%)
Any craps	(11.1%)
3 or 11 proposition	(11.1%)
2 or 12 proposition	(13.9%)
Any 7	(16.1%)

Oh yes, those deceptive offerings like hopping-hardways, world bets, horn bets and insurance type wagers will get you free membership, courtesy of casino management, to the tootsie-pop club.

DEAR MARK: *Why is it that when you win once, you keep betting because you believe you'll be lucky enough to win again?* **Sally O.**

Sally, I will sum it up in two words: **euphoric recall**. Far too many gamblers believe in the adage that you should never go a day without making a bet because you might be walking around lucky and not even know it.

Unfortunately, Sally, it is an inane approach to gambling that generally results in nightmarish consequences.

DEAR MARK: *How important is money management to winning in the casino?* **Steven S.**

Without hesitation, Steven, I would call money management the life or death of your casino visit. What good money management principles will do is minimize your losses and in most cases protect your winnings. Furthermore, by combining sound bets with practical money management techniques you will always maximize your chances of leaving the casino a winner.

DEAR MARK: *Could you please clear up some confusion about how the draw cards are actually dealt in video poker? Are not the five draw cards dealt at the same time as the first five cards I see on a screen?* **Frank L.**

Many players, even video poker experts, believe that the machine initially deals 10 cards: five up cards that you visually see, plus one additional card concealed underneath each card on the screen. Not true. It strictly depends, Frank, on who manufactured the video poker machine.

IGT, the largest producer of video poker machines that you will encounter in a casino, operates their equipment as follows: The first five cards are displayed, and any additional cards needed are taken from the top of the deck. But IGT is not the only manufacturer of video poker machines. There are quite a few others that engineer their machines to work in the manner you described in your question.

So, Frank, because IGT produces the most video poker machines in use, a generalized answer would be: The draw card you receive will resemble kitchen table poker where the next card being dealt is off the top of the deck.

DEAR MARK: *Could you please explain what betting limits are in a casino?* **Steve K.**

Betting limits establish both the minimum and maximum amount of money you can wager on one bet. You cannot wager less than the minimum nor more than the maximum posted on the table game. Betting limits vary from casino to casino, pit to pit and even table to table, Steve, so always look for a game within your financial resources.

♠ 55 ♠
A Nevada Perspective
from a Chaise Lounge

DEAR MARK: *I have always enjoyed reading the history of the West and the free-spirited nature of its participants. Is there any one quote that best describes a Nevadan's attitude toward life?* **Gary H.**

Former Nevada governor Grant Sawyer perhaps explained it best while stretched poolside in a lounge chair at the Flamingo. He said, "Our attitude toward life, save under the most urgent provocation, is relaxed, tolerant and mindful that if others are allowed to go on their way unmolested, a man stands a chance of getting through by himself with a minimum of irritation."

DEAR MARK: *Realizing that keno is a sucker bet, I avoid donating money to the casino. Because the game is relatively new here in New Jersey, few players know how bad the odds are. I'm curious, how long has keno been played in Nevada?* **Carl H.**

You're right, Carl. June 15, 1994, was the date the New Jersey Casino Control Commission gave legal permission to Atlantic City casino operators to pillage and loot their patrons wallets via keno.

Out here in Nevada, keno appeared in 1936 when Francis Lyden introduced the game at the Palace Club in Reno. With an initial limit of $4,000, it was called "Race Horse Keno" with names of horses assigned to each of the 80 numbers. As each game was called the numbers were announced as "jockey number 55 on the Polish Prince."

In 1951, the "Race Horse" version was dropped and the game became known simply as keno.

DEAR MARK: *What are the odds of hitting 15 straight football bets found on most parlay cards?* **Peter C.**

Plan on playing about 33,000 parlay cards, Peter. That is the odds of hitting 15 successive winning football wagers.

DEAR MARK: *Taking your advice, I now exclusively play mini-baccarat because of its low house edge. Per your past column, I do avoid the tie wager and strictly bet back and forth between the bank and player hand. I'm about to make a trip to Las Vegas and was told that somewhere downtown one casino offers better odds if you bet the bank hand. Where is it?* **Maggie C.**

Betting the bank hand at Binion's Horseshoe is where you get your decisive break. By lowering the commission to four percent on winning bank hands (compared to the standard five percent), the house edge drops to .6%, making it one of the better bets in Nevada.

DEAR MARK: *I am making my first trip to Las Vegas the early part of next year, not to gamble, but for a convention. Where do you recommend I book reservations?* **Robin T.**

I'm asked all the time where I like to stay when visiting Las Vegas. Tough call, but if forced to pick one place, it would be the Rio Suite Hotel. And I'm not the only one who feels this way. Zagat Hotel and Restaurant Survey has given the Rio numerous awards like best rooms, best dining, best service and best overall in Las Vegas. The Rio has also earned the ranking of "the best" in 10 categories in the Las Vegas Review-Journal most recent "Best of Las Vegas Survey."

DEAR MARK: *On the weekends when the table limits get prohibitively high for my bankroll, I retreat to video blackjack. There used to be a few video blackjack machines on the riverboats but now they're all gone. What's the low limit player to do?* **Jason M.**

Even though live blackjack is the most popular table game in the casino, video blackjack slots were some of the worst performing machines on the riverboats.

Most have been replaced by other machines that feed the casino coffers more. They still exist if you find a Bally's Game Maker multi-game machine. On the Game Maker, of all the assorted video games, blackjack tends to get the most play. Go figure.

♠ 56 ♠
Casino Loyalty Deserves
Slot Club Compensation

DEAR MARK: *I understand the latest rave in slot play is joining a slot club. Numerous casino slot hosts continue to approach me asking if I would be interested in participating. I don't want to waste my time filling out applications, but, I reward myself by searching out 9/6 video poker machines that pay a decent return. Am I missing something?* **George R.**

Missing something? Yes! Just by being a certified card-carrying member of a slot club you can receive up to a one percent cash rebate while playing video poker. On a full-pay Jacks or better 9/6 video poker machine with an expected return of 99.6%, you now command a positive expectation of 100.1%. Yes, George, this is a mathematical edge against a cybernetic one-armed bandit the whole time you're playing.

Though the equation for perks differs from casino to casino, this is what I typically receive with my Tropicana's Island Winner Club card after eight hours of play on a 25¢ video poker machine: four free meal comps, a $60 room discount and at least an $80 cash rebate. In addition, they send me goodies in the mail—two-for-one buffet coupons, room discounts, invitations to casino events and even free gifts. The Tropicana pays me for my loyalty. And what are you getting? ZIPPO!

In the future, George, make yourself a sought-after guest. Simply fill out as many slot club application cards as you can get your hands on and start making the casinos compete for your business. Join me in the VIP line at the buffet.

DEAR MARK: *What are some of the advantages the casino holds over the player in blackjack?* **Bart D.**

The ONLY advantage the casino has over the player in blackjack is that the casino plays last. If you bust and so does the dealer, the house already has your money in the tray. Player skills, or lack of them, are really what are going to determine your success in a casino. The casino, Bart, doesn't beat you; it merely gives you the opportunity to beat yourself.

111

DEAR MARK: *Please end a discussion among friends. When using your club card in any game machine or slot, exactly what does it track? Paper or coins in, payment out, time and date?* **R. H.**

Most casino slots today have a fully automated player tracking system, or SMART—Slot Marketing and Revenue Tracking. With the swipe of your slot club card, onboard software knows your name, address, interests, denomination of play, favorite machines, how much you have invested, your winnings at any given hour and if you have a dog named Sparky. Tell a slot host any pertinent information about yourself and it's fair game for the casino's computer database.

On the plus side, your information helps them with direct-mail campaigns informing you of promotions, upcoming slot tournaments, parties, reduced room rates, casino events and most importantly, comps, comps, comps.

Shades of 1984? Probably, but player gratuities far outweigh Big Brother knowing the date of your wedding anniversary.

DEAR MARK: *I have been going to my local casino for about six months, and I mostly play blackjack, but recently have been playing the electronic roulette machines. Is the sequence of numbers pre-programmed, or is it a random number determined by the machine at the time of the roll? Also, what is the best bet to make when playing roulette? I have seen players blanket the whole board, and some just keep betting on the same numbers until they come up.* **Barry S.**

Assuming programming integrity, all spins are random, which, Barry, is what you can expect in regulated casinos as there is no reason for the house to risk breaking the law and lose their valuable casino license by programming the machines to beat you.

As for the best bet in roulette, there really isn't any. All bets on a double zero roulette table hold the same 5.26% house advantage, with one exception; the five-number bet (0, 00, 1, 2, 3). The casino edge on that wager is 7.9%.

"Gambling is just like dram drinking; momentary excitement and wretched intervals; full consciousness of the mischievous effects of the habit and equal difficulty in abstaining from it."
– CHARLES GREVILLE, DIARIST

♠ 57 ♠
Putting Gambling and "Luck" into Perspective

DEAR MARK: *I am writing a paper on luck for a college logic class. You once wrote of individuals who had won the lottery more than once. Granted, that is lucky, but has there ever been an individual who was crowned the "luckiest person" in the world?* **Rachel G.**

Luck and logic—now there is an oxymoron if ever there was one.

Sorry, Rachel, I know of no such list of luckiness. My favorite benchmark of providential fortuitousness has to be that of Vesna Vulovic. In 1972, Vulovic was a 22-year-old flight attendant on a Yugoslav Airlines DC-9 enroute from Stockholm to Belgrade when a bomb planted by Croatian terrorists exploded on board the plane at 33,330 feet. All 27 aboard perished except for Vulovic, who by chance was the only person in the tail section of the aircraft when it fell to earth from six miles above. The rear portion of the airliner stayed intact and took a life-saving bounce by hitting a snow-covered mountain slope at a favorable angle. Vulovic lived to tell about it.

I doubt you can get luckier than that.

DEAR MARK: *I was in Las Vegas recently and made it a point to find the 9/6 jacks or better video poker machines. At one place I even found a 10/7 machine but noticed that it only paid even money on two pairs. Most of the 9/6 machines paid two for one on two pairs. Is this a case of the house giveth and the house taketh away?* **Jim D.**

Good eye, Jim. Jacks or better machines are often categorized by their payouts on the Full House and Flush lines. These are the lines the casino alters to increase and decrease the house edge. Like you, many players feel they have found a bargain when they find a 10/7 machine. But on closer examination, you'll note a bit of casino charlatanism as the even money payout for two pair lowers your return by almost 5 percent.

These machines should be avoided.

113

DEAR MARK: *Now that we are retired, my husband and I love to travel and enjoy going to different casinos in the different states we visit. Could you please recommend a guide which lists all the different casinos by state?* **Mary K.**

By far, the best all-inclusive guide of casinos nationwide is Steve Bourie's, *American Casino Guide*. Updated yearly, the 1999 American Casino Guide indexes every casino/resort in the U.S., plus all the toll-free phone numbers, web sites and e-mail addresses. Bourie also lists which casinos give away the Fun Books, the marketing department's phone number so you can stay on top of slot clubs, more than 200 pages of casino gambling tips, techniques and winning strategies, a comprehensive listing of room and suite rates, riverboat cruise schedules and cost, buffet prices and detailed maps. Additionally, you get more than $900 in valuable casino coupons.

You can find the 1999 American Casino Guide at all major bookstores for $14.95, or call Bourie direct at (800) 741-1596.

DEAR MARK: *This is how I accrue my "gambling money." I never spend change. I throw all my change into a bag at the end of the day and periodically roll it and take it to the bank and exchange it for bills. This is my "play money" when I go to Las Vegas or Lake Tahoe. All my winnings add to this fund, and conversely, losses also come from this fund. Just thought I would pass along this tip.* **Craig S.**

You're singing from the right pew, Craig. Loose change gambling is responsible, disciplined gambling. I applaud you, Craig, for gambling with money "you can afford to lose."

Two archaeologists were digging out in the desert when they came across ancient human remains. After a swift examination, one turned to the other and said,
"This man definitely committed suicide."
"How can you tell?" asked his companion.
"Well, he has a note clutched in his hand.
It says 5,000 shekels on Goliath!"

♠ 58 ♠
Slot Machines Don't Have
Synthetic Reasoning Cababilities

DEAR MARK: *Does the slot machine know once I've won three or four small jackpots in a row to stop paying me because it has already paid me too much money?* **Roger B.**

The machines are not programmed to say to themselves; "Oh no, I've been paying Roger way too much money. Time to stiff this loser." Slot machines, Roger, do not operate by artificial intelligence as you suggest in your question, but are preprogrammed to pay out a certain percentage on a random basis with all kinds of streaks—good and bad—appearing. All symbols are selected by a random number generator (RNG) and this small internal chip knows nothing about cycles. What the programming does tell the casino operators is that after millions and millions of decisions, "X" amount of money will be earned by the casino and lost by the players.

But no one, Bob, not even the machine, knows what the actual "sequence" of wins and losses will be.

DEAR MARK: *Is it true that in Canadian casinos there is no tax taken from jackpots?* **Randal H.**

True, Randal, all winnings are passed on to the player. But, American players like you who play at Casino Niagara and win more than $10,000 are required to report it at the border.

DEAR MARK: *Recently a dealer flipped over a blackjack and yelled out "red snapper." Is that some sort of insider lingo? I've never heard it before.* **Noreen R.**

A snapper is an archaic term for blackjack. A red snapper is a blackjack composed of two red cards.

DEAR MARK: *Is it true that baccarat is a very erratic, risky game and the casinos bottom line can be in jeopardy by a high roller?* **John Z.**

If ever, John, there were a scenario where a casino owner would climb to the top of his casino and leap, it would be when a whale—a heavy hitter who has just as much money as the casino—sits down on a baccarat game and begins kicking rear end.

For the bigger joints in Las Vegas, baccarat represents a large percentage of their annual win. But baccarat can be extremely volatile, both in volume and in the casino's hold percentage.

What's interesting is that only a small number of high rollers contribute to the total baccarat revenue. It is estimated that the very highest of high rollers (those with credit limits of more than $1 million and the potential for $1 billion annually in casino play) number no more than 200 planetwide. So why do they play baccarat? Because of the game's intensity—40 to 60 hands an hour—and its favorable odds—under 1.25% for the house. I've seen single bets on a baccarat game at $100,000 a whack. Hoo ahh! Multiply that by 50 hands per hour and you have $5,000,000 in play that could possibly swing against the house. Too bad, so sad, the megabucks sheik from Saudi Arabia is glad.

Given the above factors, baccarat's high betting limits and favorable odds to the player, yes, John, it is a very risky and unpredictable game for the casino.

DEAR MARK: *While playing blackjack, if the dealer miscounts the player's total and starts to pay off on a losing hand, is the player expected to correct the dealer?* **Lane B.**

The short answer is no. You do not have to inform the dealer that he has made a payoff mistake. When I pitched cards, players never informed me that I had made an error (of course I'm exaggerating just a little bit, but that's how I remember it!).

Nevertheless, Lane, virtue, honesty, even altering your karma comes into play. Only you can decide where your integrity lies.

"The Bellagio in Las Vegas would be the hotel that God would build, if he had the money." – STEVE WYNN

♠ 59 ♠
Casino Management Can't Mandate Cheerfulness

DEAR MARK: *I have cut and collected every column that you have written. We really enjoy them here in Biloxi, Mississippi. My one complaint is that in a few columns you use the phrase "certified friendly" when it comes to dealers. To be honest with you, I've run across some real boorish ones. What constitutes, in your opinion, "certified friendly"?* **Raymond G.**

Raymond, it could be something as simple as management forcing dealers to wear ridiculous "stinkin badges" that pronounce that they are certified friendly. Dealers who are subject to such autocratic casino marketing plans will tell you that other, more savory adjectives could also be applied.

A specific example would be at Station Casinos in Las Vegas where they have a "10-5" rule for blackjack dealers. Dealers on dead tables are expected to show their pearly whites to any prospective player who comes within 10 feet of their game. Any player who comes within 5 feet of their tables is to be verbally greeted.

Will any of this make a crabby dealer more like Snuggles, the Fabric Softener Bear? Hardly. Casino management can try to legislate geniality, but being a friendly dealer, of which there are many, comes from within. You can't decree friendliness.

DEAR MARK: *I visited Las Vegas for the first time in August and had the time of my life learning to play craps at the Imperial Palace. They had 50¢ minimum bets and 100X odds. With the fact that I was winning, and they kept bringing me drinks, it was a fun and an inexpensive learning experience. My question is, does the 100X odds benefit the player by reducing the house advantage any more than a single or double odds game?* **Chris S.**

117

Yes, Chris, considerably. BUT, if your bankroll is undercapitalized, after a few bad rolls your typical weekend gambler will be wiped out. Even on a 50¢ game.

A crap game that offers 100X odds is for players who typically wager between $25-$50 per hand, not a 50¢ inexperienced player. It takes nerve, and capital, to put $50.50 on the line and wait for a 4 to roll.

DEAR MARK: *My brother-in-law thinks he can make a living counting cards while playing blackjack. He's been playing on low limit tables because he doesn't have any money. I have a two-part question. First, can he really beat the casino with his small bankroll, and second, if he can actually beat the casino counting cards, why does the casino offer a game they can't make any money at?* **Robert A.**

Because casinos make their money from the uninformed masses (over 95 percent), and what the heck, throw in bad card counters as well.

Card counters in general have an inherent advantage of between .5 and 1.5 percent against the house. But in your brother-in-law's case, even if his debatable skills rival the pros, because his bankroll is limited (e.g., $1000 or less), his slight edge will produce nothing more than a $5-an-hour job for him.

Is it worth the constant hassle from pit bosses, exposure of his bankroll and the possibility of financial ruin for $5 an hour? I'll pass and let him decide.

DEAR MARK: *I recently came across a game in a casino that looked very similar to the game of War that we used to play as kids. Both players received one card and the high card won. What's the catch?* **Ronald B.**

Yes, Ronald, called War, this is a variation of the same senseless game you played as a youngster on the kitchen table. Both you and the dealer each receive one card, and the high card wins. In the event that both cards are equal, you must double your initial bet, and two more cards are dealt. Again the high card wins; however, you win only your original wager. This is how the casino pickpockets your billfold. The casino advantage from this one rule change: 7.14%.

Thumbs down for War.

♠ 60 ♠
Rip-off on the Midway?

DEAR MARK: *Your column Do two-year-olds gamble? You bet! was terrific. But 25¢ at the local supermarket for an egg with a cheap toy inside is nothing compared to the amount I spend on my grandchildren on the midway. Last summer I must have spent more than $40 at one carnival trying to knock down two coke bottles with a softball. I got nothing, I mean nothing. Talk about games being rigged.* **Harold C.**

Not all games, Harold, are rigged, or all carnival workers crooked; but all "honest" games are designed to favor the game operator. Like the casino, that's how they make their money. Just because you lost doesn't mean you were swindled.

There are three basic types of games that can be found on the midway. A skill game, a flat game and a game of chance. Two of the three are illegal. Only a game of skill, in which you have the ability through human proficiency to control the final outcome, is legal at a carnival.

A flat is a game where you have no chance of winning no matter how dexterous you are. Harold, you could have been a past singles champion on the PBA tour and you still couldn't knock those bottles over. The game is surreptitiously controlled by the game operator—which may have occurred at the carnival you attended.

Chance games involve no control over the final outcome. A chance game is also illegal because it's gambling, which, without a gaming license, is prohibited in all states. Remember the gambling formula, Harold? Courts have found that every gambling apparatus must consist of three components: consideration, chance and prize. You pay something of value (consideration) to play; you receive something of value (prize), usually more than the amount bet; and the outcome depends on chance. Because leveling coke bottles should be based solely on skill, not chance, this is what separates it from a gambling device.

Coke Roll, the game you mentioned in your question, consists of two coke bottles set up on a platform five feet away. The object is to roll the ball down the platform and knock both standing coke bottles over with one ball. Note, Harold, that the ball you were given is not a regulation softball but one that is much lighter in weight. Without defying the law of physics, the only way you could have won is to hit both bottles directly in the center at the same time.

Because there is no easy way for an unsuspecting mark to detect if the game was rigged, my best guess is that you were playing a flat game and the operator gaffed the challenge. Gaffing is to fix, cheat or rig a game by using misdirection, sleight of hand or any secret cheating device.

Coke Roll can be gaffed by a deceptive carny simply by off-setting one of the coke bottles. This moves the center of the bottles off to one side, making the second bottle impossible to hit with an underweight softball. By hitting only one bottle, that bottle will absorb most of the ball's energy, leaving nothing left to knock down bottle two. Consequently, bye-bye $40.

A dear friend of mine, blessed with genetics that make her look 20 years younger than she truly is, loves to beat the midway cadre out of prizes because they can never guess her age. But does she truly win? She gives the barker a dollar and he tries to guess her birth date. If he wins he keeps her dollar; and if he loses, he keeps her dollar and gives her a prize worth 25¢. Honest? Yes! Highway robbery? Yes!

"In the queer mess of human destiny the determining factor is luck. For every important place in life there are many men of fairly equal capacities. Among them luck decides who shall accomplish the great work, who shall be crowned with laurel, and who shall fall back into silence and obscurity."
– WILLIAM E. WOODWARD

♠ 61 ♠
Compounding Money Only Works on Wall Street

DEAR MARK: *On a certain 25¢ video poker machine that I like to play, the machine allows me to double up what I've just won by picking high or low against a pair of rolling dice. This really can't be a good bet, right?* **Nancy R.**

For those of you who don't know it, some video poker machines offer you the option of risking your current winning hand for a chance at doubling your money. Though it can be high/low against a machine-dealt playing card, in Nancy's case, it's against a simulated dice roll (2-6 under, 7 push, 8-12 over).

At first glance, Nancy, many players believe this is just another way for the casino to pillage your purse. Not so, my friend. It 's actually one of the best bets in the casino. No house edge means a 50-50 chance of you doubling your money. Sound too good to be true? Yes and no.

Though each decision has exactly a 50-50 chance, the odds of winning more than one in a row will decline sharply. Experts are divided on whether you're gambling on individual rolls or a sequence of rolls (myself in the latter category), but either way, the bet is heavily stacked against you if your goal is to string 10 wins together. Also, don't plan on doubling as often as you wish. We all think of the possibilities, Nancy, like winning 19 hands in a row with a $2.50 investment and becoming an instant millionaire. Unfortunately, just like the table games where table limits apply, the compounding of money by parlaying winnings won't work here either. Machines limit the doubling from as little as five times in a row to 10,000 coins returned ($2,500).

So the long and short of it, Nancy, is to show some strong money management (cash control) and play this wager without going overboard.

121

DEAR MARK: *I was on the Internet looking for information on casino gambling for a school project. My topic is called "Should the United States Promote Casino Gambling?" I found your column called "Covering All the Bases" very helpful. I was wondering if you had any other material that might help.* **Lynne T.**

Because of limited space, Lynne, allow me to temporarily stand neutral on the proliferation of gambling across America and the government's active participation in it. For those who want a phenomenal research treatise on your legislature's relationships with the gambling industry, look to Robert Goodman's book *The Luck Business*, subtitled, "The Devastating Consequences and Broken Promises of America's Gambling Explosion."

Besides your school project, I would highly recommend this solid study to all government policymakers and voters alike who will decide in the future whether the fastest growing industry in the nation (gambling) belongs in their neighborhood.

With half of America now living within two hours of casino gambling, it's sooner than you think.

DEAR MARK: *Recently I was on a crap game where the dice were rolling numbers for eight hours. Not non-stop, but it was a player's game and I just couldn't leave. Good thing I didn't. I bought in for $100, played just like you recommended (pass line bets with odds, placing the 6 and 8), and walked out eight hours later with $3,400. I thought your readers might appreciate that every now and then, even the small-time player, has a night worth remembering.* **Clark D.**

Bosses give you the heave-ho, relatives disown you, friends forget you, but an unbelievable night on a crap game, ah, that lasts forever.

Thanks for sharing, Clark.

"Gambling is the future on the internet.
You can only look at so many dirty pictures."
– SIMON NOBLE, AN AUSTRIAN-BASED INTERNET BOOKMAKER

♠ 62 ♠
Mission Accomplished

DEAR MARK: *I go to Atlantic City about two times a month, stay overnight and lose a bundle. I just love it. My question: I play a "Reel-em-in" 25-cent slot machine. Now you can bet up to 45 quarters on these machines. Well, after losing so much money, I found these same machines in the nickel denomination. Now I find that I can play 45 nickels and it is only $2.25 a hand compared to $11.25 a hand on quarter machines. Would it be better to play a dollar slot with 2 coins in ($2) or play the nickels at $2.25 with 45 nickels in? Same with the quarter slots. Play with 45 quarters at $11.25 a hand or play a $5 slot with 2 coins in ($10.00)? I always thought the higher the denomination machine, the better your chances of winning. Please give me your feedback.* **Loretta K.**

You have many questions, Loretta, but let's start with "lose a bundle and just loving it." I can't help but think: are you really having fun when you're losing? Taken as known, the casino has but two goals: separate you from your money and put a smile on your face. Evidently with you they have achieved their objective.

Your style of play creates this scenario. Insert multiple coins, play for a short while, lose, go home.

Essentially, you are aggravating an already bad situation by risking more, at a much faster rate, on a game with a high negative expectation. For every dollar you insert, Loretta, the casino is going to keep around nine cents, and it doesn't matter whether you pump in 5 or 45 quarters. This is a certainty for two reasons. First, slot machines are pre-programmed to return a certain percentage to the player and second, New Jersey casinos, by law, make public the average percent of each wager that is returned to the player.

123

Quarter machines (25¢) in Atlantic City return on average 90.5 cents of each dollar played compared to 91.7 on a dollar machine. Hardly a break on the Jersey Shore when you bump up to a higher denomination machine.

Furthermore, weigh the 90.5¢ return on Jersey's quarter machines against the following gaming jurisdictions and you'll notice that Atlantic City slot machines are no bargain: Colorado 94.1; Illinois 92.4; Iowa 92.4; Nevada 94.7.

My gambling recommendation to you is as follows. Bet a whole lot less, like nickel or quarter machines with a five coin maximum, or make nominal wagers on some of the smarter bets I suggest weekly in this column. Then, write me back and let me know how much more you enjoy gambling when you break even for a trip or, better yet, actually win and put a few of the casino's dollars in your purse.

DEAR MARK: *I would like to know the correct basic strategy play for a soft 18. I learned that when one has an ace/seven, the smart play is to stand on a dealer's 2, 7, 8, and hit all others. With my limited mathematical skills, I have come to accept this as correct. However, I still get looks from dealers when I play out the hand. What do you think?* **Steve L.**

Your play is nearly correct.

An ace-seven is one of those tricky hands about which numerous experts disagree. The general consensus is to stand on 2, 7, 8; double down when playing rules allow it against a 3-6; and hit against a 9 or 10 count card. But against an ace the pros are nearly divided between hitting and standing. I side with the half that recommends hitting versus standing when fronting an ace.

♠ 63 ♠
Casinos Don't Mind
an Infrequent Winner

DEAR MARK: *I watched a gentleman on a blackjack table start with $100 and beat the casino out of $4,500. It didn't even faze the pit boss. I realize it wasn't his money but shouldn't he have been more concerned that someone beat the casino out of $4,500 with so little invested?* **Rob B.**

If the game is square, the casino shouldn't give one iota when someone wins a huge sum of money, even if he or she started with a meager bankroll. It is not all that rare for a player to take a hundred dollar bill and run it up to four digits.

Casino operators realize they will suffer short term losing streaks, even when every bet is in their favor. Besides, Rob, casinos are retail establishments. If none of the customers had any chance of winning big, how long do you think they could keep their doors open? They actually prefer a few winners. Winners tell the 90 plus percent who lose where they won it.

The way casinos guard against financial ruin during a player's winning streak is to set betting limits at the table. It is the "house limit" that protects the casino bankroll against a lucky assault by a hot gambler. Additionally, the house knows the longer you gamble, the more exposure you have to the casino's inescapable casino edge.

The gambler's biggest advantage against the house, Rob, is to quit on your own terms, not the casino's. Unfortunately, few have the internal fortitude to take the money and run.

DEAR MARK: The reason I enjoy your column so much is because of your insider's *view. You spent 18 years in the business. No other gaming columnist I've read has. Was writing about casino gaming an afterthought?* **Marshall G.**

Someone once asked Nobel Prize winner William Faulkner for his advice to a young and struggling writer; he responded that the young person should get a job as a janitor in a whorehouse. I went into casino gambling instead—it paid more.

125

DEAR MARK: *Does the Megabucks machine that has a jackpot of $1,252,000 and continually climbing in Reno have the exact same jackpot in Las Vegas?* **Jim K.**

Yes, Jim, they are exactly the same.

Megabucks is a statewide network of progressive slot carousels linked together to produce huge, dramatic jackpots. It was created by IGT to challenge the big payoffs found in state lotteries.

Each slot machine in the Megabucks network plays independently. A small computer chip in each machine monitors every coin played and communicates that information electronically to a mainframe computer at IGT's headquarters in Reno. The central computer keeps track of every Megabucks slot and maintains a constant tally of the jackpot. Then the computer projects the ever-changing jackpot total to all Megabuck units where it is displayed on the digital tote board.

DEAR MARK: *The last time I went to Las Vegas was in 1963. In December I'm going back to see what all the hoopla is about. One problem; I'm a low-limit gambler. Do nickel machines still exist?* **Marge G.**

You're in luck, Marge. Low rollers can still enjoy the city of Lost Wages. There are 5,000 nickel machines at the Strip mega-resorts and 4,200 downtown.

DEAR MARK: *It hasn't happened to me yet, but what should I do if I'm ever dealt a natural royal flush? I think I will panic and push the discard button by mistake.* **Beverly M.**

If your hand of destiny has been naturally dealt, immediately press all five hold buttons, followed by the draw button. Still nervous, Beverly? Fear not. If any of the top three hands are dealt naturally, most machines automatically skip to the payoff mode, eliminating the possibility of you hitting the wrong buttons.

♠ 64 ♠
Mistakes Shouldn't Cause Problems

DEAR MARK: *I was in Atlantic City last week minding my own business on a blackjack game, when a player started verbally insulting me on how I played my hands. He told me I was ruining his hands and always taking the dealer's bust card. Do I really have that much control over the outcome of the game?* **Helen L.**

First, Helen, it's your money, not theirs, so you should be able to play your hand any way you want. Second, one of the biggest fallacies in all of gambling is that your play affects the overall outcome of all hands dealt. Not true! Each card comes out of the shoe randomly and since you, the dealer, fellow players and yes, even the nitwit who insulted you, have no idea what the next card is, poor play will have no consequence on the game in general. Unfortunately, it does influence the outcome of "your hand," which leads me to third—playing perfect basic strategy.

Blackjack is a unique casino game because it allows players to make playing decisions that will affect the outcome of their bet. Poor play will allow the casino to have a 4-5% edge over the average player. If however you learn perfect basic strategy, that edge can be reduced to well under 1%, making it a terrific wager and one of the best player bets in the casino.

Now if the thought of breaking even against the house does not offer you ample monetary incentive to take the time to learn basic strategy, maybe knowing that you will place yourself in the 99th percentile among all players will, as less than one in every 100 players uses perfect basic strategy. Helen, your goal should be to join the one percent who do take advantage of this lucrative way of wagering.

127

DEAR MARK: *On a crap game, why is the dealer insistent that I make $6 wagers when I want to place either the 6 or 8?* **Jeff T.**

Because by betting $6 you will get the correct return for your money. When making a place bet on the 6 or 8, you should always wager in multiplies of $6 ($12, $18, $24, etc.). The reason is that 6 and 8 pay off at 7 to 6—win $7 for every $6 bet.

Anything less and the dealer will round down and you will be short changed.

DEAR MARK: *In blackjack, I seem to lose more hands than I win, even when I play perfect basic strategy against the house. If the house has only a slight edge against the player who uses basic strategy, why don't I win close to 50 percent of my hands?* **Jason C.**

If you employ perfect basic strategy, Jason, expect to win approximately 43 percent of all blackjack hands, lose 47 percent and tie 9 percent of the time. Throw out the ties, and that figure changes to winning 47 percent and losing 53 percent of hands dealt.

So how is it possible to be on even keel with the casino when you lose more hands than you win? Because some winning hands are blackjacks where you are paid 1.5 times your initial bet, or hands that you split or double down on that double your initial wager.

With losing hands you are normally betting and losing only your original bet. It is the blackjacks, double downs and splits that take you fiscally from red to the black in blackjack action. That, Jason, is why you can win as much money from 47 percent of your hands than from the casino-captured 53 percent.

"True luck consists not in holding the best of cards at the table: Luckiest is he who knows just when to rise and go home."
– JOHN HAY, AMERICAN STATESMAN

♠ 65 ♠
Cat and Mouse

DEAR MARK: *Is card counting illegal?* **Frank R.**

Frank, is using your brain illegal? No. Unfortunately, when it comes to card counting, the casino would prefer you check your brain at the front door. So though not illegal, what the casino can and will do is bar the counter from playing and back you off the game. If you're going to play this cat and mouse game to gain a one percent plus advantage, expect a pit bull (boss) to come and pleasantly say, "Frank, we appreciate your patronage but we're going to ask you to stop playing blackjack here. Feel free to play any of the other table games we offer." (Yeah, like games that have a house advantage higher than the interest rate you pay on your Visa card.)

Fortunately, Frank, not all casinos bar counters. Atlantic City, by law, cannot run you off. Instead, they impose tougher blackjack rules, multi-deck games and limit deck penetration to keep the skilled counter at bay.

Though many in the industry believe the casino has every right to back off proficient players, I personally feel the minuscule amounts lost to card counters are trivial compared to the money made from the uninformed masses of poor players—not to mention bad counters.

DEAR MARK: *Before going to Las Vegas my sister filled out a dummy keno ticket and asked me to play it 20 times. On it she had the number 55 circled by itself and the numbers 10 and 20 circled together. Each ticket cost $3. What exactly was I playing?* **Joe C.**

It's called a combination ticket, meaning different proposition bets on one keno ticket. The singular number circled, 55, was her "king number," which was to be played in combination with the other two numbers, plus played alone. She was playing a one spot (55), a two spot (10 and 20), and one three spot (10, 20 and 55).

129

DEAR MARK: *Basic strategy in blackjack dictates that I hit a soft 18 (A-7) against a 9, 10 count card or an ace. I feel a soft 18 is powerful enough and will take my occasional licks against the dealer who turns over a better hand. What would you recommend I do with a soft 18?* **Alison B.**

HIT IT.

If, Alison, in my mythical casino, which I'll call "22 Always WINS," I gave you the opportunity to automatically be dealt an 18 on each and every hand of blackjack, would you sit down and play? Not so fast my friend. For every one million hands of 18 my certified friendly dealers deal you, you will lose 280 more hands than you would win. Small spuds yes, but it tells you that 18's a losing hand over the long haul. This is why basic strategy cards advise hitting a soft 18 in certain situations.

DEAR MARK: *Most dealers, friends and even you advise against taking insurance in blackjack. How about when I have a 20 and I'm playing on a single deck game? I hate losing when I have such a strong hand.* **Stuart M.**

Question to you, Stuart: Who is holding at least two of the cards the dealer needs to make their blackjack? YOU. Insuring a hand composed of two 10 cards on a single deck game gives the house a 14.3% edge, making this one of the worst bets in the casino.

DEAR MARK: *Why is it so important to hit to a 17 when the dealer shows a 7 through ace? I tend to stay on my 15s and 16s and avoid busting. Is this a correct strategy?* **Beth B.**

The dealer's chances of having a 17 or more when he shows a 7, 8, 9, 10 or ace are between 74% and 83%. Correct basic strategy dictates that you always hit your 15 or 16.

♠ 66 ♠
Mutual Funds Versus Blackjack

DEAR MARK: *I've always felt that being in the stock market is the same as playing blackjack. They're both gambling. I might as well do something I love instead of giving some investment company my money to flush down the toilet. You're in gambling, do you agree?* **Ralph G.**

Your analysis of comparing the stock market to blackjack is way off the mark. Entering the world of blackjack as a profession (investment) takes enormous work and you're playing against, if not for a better term, a financial institution that not only has a built-in house edge but is there exclusively to beat you. Come on, Ralph. How many people do you know who win at blackjack—consistently? Compare that to what a market like NASDAQ has done over the past 10 years. Gone up, up, up! Give me a dart board and the *Wall Street Journal* and I would have averaged 12% over the past 30 years.

I'm sure your next argument will be that of becoming a sophisticated card counter. Sorry, it's not worth spending hours in smoke-filled casinos, performing tedious mental calculations and disguising your play so you won't be thrown out—just for a one percent edge.

Finally, Dr. Edward Thorp, who wrote the classic *Beat the Dealer* was, as a professional, in the investment business. Even he conceded it is far easier to make money in the financial markets than at blackjack. Unfortunately, gambling is a poor man's way of investing, and even for the poorest of investors, a $500 wager in a mutual fund is a much better bet.

131

DEAR MARK: *When the state lotto gets over $20 million here in California, my mother wants me to buy $10 worth of lottery tickets and then mail them back to her in Michigan. Is it legal for me to mail her the tickets?* **Roberta G.**

Congratulate your mother for me, Roberta, for waiting till the lottery reaches $20 million before she purchases her tickets. Because the true odds of hitting the California lottery are 18,009,460 to 1, she's actually playing the game smart.

As for the legality of sending tickets through the mail, sorry, Roberta, using the United States Postal Service for this particular ruse is against the law. Millions do it, unknowingly, but I have yet to hear of one individual who has been charged, or convicted for sending lottery tickets by mail; NOT ONE! But if you want to play it straight, it's perfectly legal to use a service like Federal Express or Airborne Express.

Where individuals and businesses have gotten into trouble is soliciting you to play a foreign lottery. Ever get one of those plain white envelopes enticing you to play the Canadian Lottery, Roberta? Don't! It's against the law, again for the same reason. U.S. Postal regulations state that using the U.S. mail to solicit people to play the lottery, or even to distribute any type of lottery material, is strictly illegal.

By the way, there's a reason why their envelope on the outside doesn't give away what's on the inside. With a Canadian Lotto return address, it would be confiscated by the USPS before it reached you.

DEAR MARK: *On a recent trip to Branson, Missouri, I stopped along the way in Kansas City and gambled for the first time. I was surprised to see both loss limits and two-hour cruises. Is that common?* **Bill K.**

The loss limits and cruise times are in place to prevent problem gamblers from spending more than they can afford to lose. Currently Missouri is the only state with these restrictions. It is the wisdom of the Missouri legislature that by setting limits you won't blow your trip bankroll, you will have time to get religion and still have enough money to see Wayne Newton in Branson.

132

♣ 67 ♣
Playing Nickel Machines
with Small Stakes

DEAR MARK: *I hate to ask this question because so many people consider keno machines to be losers. However, I do not do all that bad playing keno. Although I play table blackjack and slot machines (very selective), I still love video keno. I can sit at a nickel keno machine through an afternoon and evening. I pocket my winnings and continue to play with my original bankroll. Knowing your interests and that readers probably concentrate on table games, what are your thoughts on 5¢ keno?* **Vicki C.**

Understand, Vicki, that nickel slots are a tough beat because of their high casino hold. Consequently, they profit the house more than higher denomination machines. Table games and selected casino wagers, played intelligently, offer the greatest hope for the player whose sole purpose is walking out of the casino with the casino's loot.

But I give credence to the "entertainment factor" of gambling, especially with games (nickel machines) that are enjoyable to play on a modest bankroll (under $20). I have never been one to be critical of any player who limits his or her gambling to nickel machines. By playing solely nickels, you are in total control of your bankroll, plus you can enjoy casino gambling while limiting your cash outlay.

Also, Vicki, given a choice, it is better to play video keno versus regular keno. Besides being inexpensive to play at 5¢ a pop, video keno does not give as large an edge to casinos.

133

DEAR MARK: *When I applied for my slot club card at a casino, the slot host told me that all points were based on "coin-in" machines. What was she talking about?* **Karen K.**

When you insert your slot club card into a slot machine, the magnetic strip enables the casino to know exactly how much money you are actually betting. "Coin-in" machines count the total amount of your coins inserted, then fund your slot club card with comp points without distinguishing between remaining credits played or coins inserted.

DEAR MARK: *I loved to play this one particular machine at my favorite casino in Reno. The best way I can describe it is that it has a frog on the front of it. I called it my "little froggie." On my last trip the machine was no longer there. When I inquired what happened to the machine, I was told by someone in the slot department that the machine was not performing up to expectations. What did he mean?* **Beverly K.**

From the casino's point of view, your beloved froggie didn't hop, skip or jump all the way to the bank.

All machines, Beverly, need to show reasonable results or their replacement is inevitable. A gaming machine's performance is measured by two factors: the amount of coins wagered daily ("coin in") and the amount collected daily by the casino ("win"). If a machine's performance falters ever so slightly, a slot manager could decide a change is needed in the slot mix, meaning the placement and positioning of machines on the casino floor.

DEAR MARK: *Next month I'm going to London, England. I've planned a few hours of relaxation and would like to try my luck at the slot machines in their casinos. Any recommendations?* **Calvin R.**

Realize, Calvin, that by being a punter across the pond you will need a special membership to enter London casinos. The waiting period for a membership is 24 hours. Another shortcoming is that all casinos in London are limited by law to just six slot machines. Plan on waiting, and waiting and waiting to lose your money.

Furthermore, Calvin, your slot strategy shouldn't blueprint breaking the bank. The maximum jackpot is limited to 300 pounds of sterling, or $450.

♠ 68 ♠
Always Think Two Percent or Less

DEAR MARK: *You mentioned in a previous column that players should never make a hard way bet on a crap game. Why not?* **Norman G.**

Hey, Norman, what is Mark Pilarski's rule number one of casino gambling? (Actually, it's rule number two as rule number one is: "Only bet what you can afford to lose.") Rule number two of my gambling commandments is "Only make wagers that have less than a two percent house advantage." Hard way bets are much, much higher and will gourmandize most of your hard-earned, hopefully disposable, income.

The true odds of a hard 6 or 8 materializing are 10 to 1, but your friendly casino is only going to pay you a paltry 9 to 1. This gives the casino a 9.09 percent edge. As for the hard 4 or 10, the true odds are 8 to 1, but the payoff is a measly 7 to 1, giving the casino a whopping 11.1 percent advantage.

My advice is to stick with a pass/come bet with odds or placing the six or eight.

DEAR MARK: *My brother-in-law loves to play the "odd" bet on a roulette table. Recently in Las Vegas it came up 15 times in a row for him. What are the chances of that happening?* **Tony G.**

You didn't specify, Tony, if it was a double or a single zero roulette wheel. Because I advise my readers to play on only the latter, a single zero game, the odds would have been 50,000 to 1 of "odd" rolling 15 consecutive times. My personal all-time record when I dealt the game was 20 straight spins with black appearing. Odds: 1 in 1.8 million.

DEAR MARK: *Every Thursday I take my great grandmother to a local bingo parlor. Seems this is the most enjoyable time we have together. She told me that she used to mark her bingo card with kernels of corn. I didn't realize the game was that old. How old is bingo and where did it originate?* **Sally C.**

Bingo's beginnings, Sally, have never been truly authenticated, but the game was made popular by Edwin S. Lowe, a traveling salesman who accidentally chanced upon the game at a carnival in Atlanta in 1929.

You revealed, Sally, that your great grandmother used corn to mark her card; well, don't forget to tell your bingo-bonding matriarch that the game was originally called Beano because it was played by covering the numbers with beans.

DEAR MARK: *Is it legal to chart the rolls on a roulette table and then bet accordingly?* **Justin G.**

According to what, Justin? Any attempts to impose numerical precision on a game that insists upon remaining imprecise is futile. It is permissible to "chart" the results of spins in an attempt to identify and exploit streaks, but because each spin is an independent event, no previous results have any bearing on what happens in the future.

DEAR MARK: *You once wrote that no one has ever hit a solid 14 or 15 spot in Nevada. How about my unlucky 13-spot ticket. Anybody ever hit a solid 13 spot?* **Martha R.**

Conclusively, I have no documentation one way or the other, and believe me, Martha, I've been searching. My guesstimate would be that no one ever has. But here's a sobering thought that you can check out for yourself next time you're in downtown Reno. At Fitzgeralds, take the escalator from the first to the second floor and you will find hanging on their wall of fame pictures of winning keno tickets through the 90s. The highest ticket hit so far this decade was a nine spot, and surprisingly, just one.

What does that tell you, Martha?

♠ 69 ♠
Plastic or Paper

DEAR MARK: *During conversation with one of the many rotating poker dealers at the Horseshoe in Boosier City, he mentioned that the cards they used for poker were essentially indestructible because they were plastic and theoretically can handle a lifetime of use. What is your experience in dealing them, and why are they not used in all table games as opposed to just poker?* **John R.**

The United States Player Card Co. of Cincinnati, Ohio manufactures the majority of cards used in casinos across America. Despite the use of high quality paper, laminating and enameling, the life of these wafer-thin pasteboard products is quite short. On average, cards are changed on a table game every hour, double decks every two and on a shoe game every shift (eight hours). Even with this limited lifespan, paper cards are substantially cheaper than their plastic counterparts and would be cost prohibitive to put on all of the casinos blackjack tables.

In poker you need cards that stand up to wear and tear as the player handles the majority of the deck every hand. Additionally, concealment of your playing hand in poker versus blackjack is an issue, plus, plastic decks in poker rooms are seldom changed during a shift.

Though plastic cards are indestructible and their durability far surpasses that of a standard playing card, they do get dirty and need a regular cleaning. In the golden days of gambling, cards were washed by hand, by dealers, with seltzer water. Now they use card washing machines.

My experience of using plastic cards is rather limited—actually only twice—when a severe snowstorm in Reno cancelled a card shipment over the Christmas holidays. This depleted the pit's inventory, and blackjack dealers used the reserve from the poker room. Because I found them much slicker than paper cards, harder to handle because of their smaller size and flimsy when shuffling, I'm not an aficionado of plastic cards.

DEAR MARK: *Over the last two years I have been on the losing streak from hell. Every slot machine I touch has been a loser. This past year alone I have lost $5,000, which I might add, is more than I can afford to donate to the casinos. My question is, when does a player finally decide enough is enough and quit playing slot machines?* **Anita J.**

Because my rule #1 of gambling is "only bet what you can afford to lose," followed by, "the smarter you play, the luckier you'll be," NOW is that time. Consider in lieu of slots, making wagers, within your means, on some of the smarter bets I suggest weekly in this column.

Correspondingly, Anita, I would be remiss if I didn't recommend finding an alternative form of entertainment. I know of one player who when her slot play went sour, rancid to the tune of $10,000 in six months, quit gambling and became what she calls a lawn hobbyist.

Now that's exchanging one form of manure for another.

DEAR MARK: *What are your thoughts on video craps?* **Michael P.**

Called Live Video Craps, this electronic version of a dice game is offered by many casinos at 25¢ a roll. Cheap, yes, but don't expect the same thrill and camaraderie as its table-game cousin on a Saturday night. Plus the game has one expensive waterloo. Excluding the 7, all numbers become the point. That includes the 2, 3, 11 and 12. This gives the house a 5% edge on your pass line bet. That, Michael, is notably higher than the 1.4% advantage the casino holds on a live game.

For familiarity of the game of craps at 25¢ a pop, OK; but wager no more.

*"Depend on the rabbit's foot if you will,
but remember it didn't work for the rabbit." –* R. E. SHAY

♠ 70 ♠
Play Where There's Competition

DEAR MARK: *Two questions, please. Do 25¢ slots pay back more than 5¢ machines? Also, does Nevada have the best slots?* **Sharon T.**

First, Sharon, let's get the easy stuff out of the way. Five-cent slots return less than 25¢ slots, which return less than $1 slots, and of course, less than the $5 machines. The reason those 5¢ slots pay you _____ (you fill in the space) is because they take the same amount of real estate in a casino as the other machines, plus cost as much, if not more (picture losers beating on them) to maintain. Oh, yes, a brief explanation of what I mean by "return." For every dollar inserted, the slot's computer is preprogrammed to give back a certain percentage to you, the player. It's that simple.

As for where to play, Nevada slots in general give you more cluck-for-the-buck, but you'll find more coins dropping in your tray anywhere casinos slug it out for customers. Like anything else, you'll benefit most where there's competition.

While we're at it, Sharon, let's examine the differences between the boats where you live, Illinois, and the gambling vessels in Iowa. Starting with the 5¢ slots, there is no competition. Illinois has only 40 nickel machines in the entire state compared to 642 in Iowa. Look for an average return of 87 percent on Iowa's 5¢ machines. As for the quarter circuit, in Illinois, expect an average payback of 91.6 percent compared to 91.8 percent across the river.

And in Nevada, if you decide to make a gaming pilgrimage out west, your best play is the 92.2 percent payback on the 5¢ machines in Reno and the 95.7 percent average return on the 25¢ slots in downtown Las Vegas.

DEAR MARK: *Can a casino, or anyone for that matter, mess with the computer chip in a slot machine so that a jackpot will never appear on the screen?* **Morgan P.**

Feel safe, Morgan, that in your state, Missouri, gaming operates under the strict Gaming Commission guidelines, insuring that every chip will deliver random action each and every time you insert a coin.

In Missouri, the Gaming Commission tests each e-prom chip (erasable programmable read only memory) when the machines are first installed to verify that the machine will operate as proposed by the casino. Then when large jackpots are hit, a Highway Patrol Officer, who is an agent of the Gaming Commission, "cobotrons" (detects if the chip has been altered) the e-prom to make sure that it hasn't been tampered with. This can amount to a dozen cobotron tests per day, per boat.

Sorry to bore you with all this nerdy computer stuff, Morgan, but I do plan a column soon on how the slots of today (computers) work—in layman's lingo that is.

DEAR MARK: *If you were limited to making just one bet in a casino and had a limited budget, what would it be?* **Bo T.**

Too easy, Bo. Since one of my greatest passions is open wheel racing, my one wager would be on the Indianapolis 500, sitting in a sportsbook for three hours sipping free cocktails and watching grown men (and woman, Lynn St. James) making left-hand turns wasting methanol.

The general public may not share the same fixation for boredom, so I would recommend plan B, a pass line wager on a craps game. Three specific reasons come to mind. First, it's a wager with a small house advantage (1.4 percent). Second, though playing perfect basic strategy at blackjack or video poker drops that casino edge even lower, a pass line bet requires limited (actually zero) knowledge. And finally, if you ask any craps player, Bo, they'll tell you craps is truly the fastest, most exhilarating game in the casino.

With low table minimums and a modest pass line bet on the layout, I would agree.

Nine gamblers could not feed a single rooster.
— YUGOSLAV PROVERB

♠ 71 ♠
A Push is NOT a Win

DEAR MARK: *When playing Video Poker, I consistently win by getting high pairs but struggle for the higher hands. Can I successfully beat the house on a high pair alone?* **Rhonda T.**

Rhonda, we need to separate the wheat from the chaff. One of the reasons video poker is so popular is that it returns your investment for a pair of jacks to aces. But, Rhonda, never consider a push a win. The psychological effect of returned coins from a push has at best, dubious value. All it does is make you feel like a winner, when in reality you're not. Treat even-money payoffs not as a win against the casino but just getting YOUR hard-earned money back.

Personally, I've always felt that this erroneous impression of winning is one of the most powerful false hope methods the casino has against you, not only with your high pair scenario but also when it's a push on a blackjack table or a one-cherry payoff on a pull handle slot machine.

So do you want to win more consistently, Rhonda? Find 9/6 video poker pay tables or 8/5 machines with progressives nearing $2,200, then play perfect basic strategy. A high pair now and then will make you consistent all right, a consistent loser.

DEAR MARK: *In Las Vegas, I saw a casino advertise that on their selected video poker machines your return can be more than 100%. Is this possible? Isn't the casino going to lose money?* **Mary S.**

Yes, Mary, the casinos would lose money if every player had unlimited access to "selected machines," plus understood and used perfect basic strategy. But because fewer than one percent effectively play perfect basic strategy, the casino won't lose money by making such an offer. You also answered part of your question by stating "on selected machines." Sometimes those "selected machines" can be as few as two on the whole casino floor. No chance of two expert players grinding away at the house and affecting the casino quarterly report. Plus, the casino will generally surround those "selected machines" with others that have pay tables offering significantly lower payoffs, guaranteeing even more winnings from the uneducated masses.

Like casino mogul Steve Wynn says, "If you wanna make money in a casino, own one."

DEAR MARK: *I have found a couple of web sites that survey blackjack conditions at various casinos and sometimes they quote a "Penetration Percentage." Exactly what is that? Is there anything a player can do to influence it?* **Dennis L.**

How many cards a dealer pitches from his deck before he shuffles is called penetration. If he deals all the cards out, that's 100 percent penetration. For the average Joe playing on the game, penetration has little significance. However, for the card counter, the depth of penetration is a key variable on whether to play on that game. The deeper a counter can go into a deck, the better.

You also asked, Dennis, if you can influence it? Sort of. Every casino has a set policy on how deep they will allow their dealers to go before they want them to shuffle-up. But casinos do have lazy dealers who don't like to shuffle. Shuffling forces them to be certified friendly and converse with the customer. Believe me, no amount of Prozac is going to get a stiff dealer yapping. One dealer told me that for 10 years, working in four different casinos, he always dealt to the bottom of the deck to avoid conversation. Not once did a pit boss or the "eye in the sky" ask him to change his rogue conduct.

By the way, that dealer is now running a casino in the Midwest.

♠ 72 ♠
Don't Quit Your Day Job

DEAR MARK: *In a past column, you stated that video poker has a return of 99 percent to the smart player and can be mathematically one of the best bets in the casino. My question is this. If I combine my passion for the game, a low house advantage and jackpots that run more than $1,000, is there any possibility that I could make a living playing video poker?* **Ted L.**

Assuming, Ted, you were to do all the right things like finding full-pay (9/6) jacks-or-better machines and play perfect basic strategy, I would still recommend the following advice. Don't quit your day job! Even though your expected payback is more than 99 percent, actually 99.544 percent, you must take into account that those high returns are based on you hitting the royal flush. And why a royal flush? Because a royal on a full pay (9/6) jacks-or-better machine accounts for 1.981 percent of your total return. Also of note, Ted, plan on playing video poker an average of 60 hours, with rapid play, before hitting a royal flush. Even a straight flush can be expected only once every six hours, and four-of-a-kind hands occur just once an hour. Those hands are significant because they represent another five percent of a player's return.

What this all means to the video poker player, Ted, is that the casino has a 10 percent advantage while you're waiting for the big payoff. Finally, Ted, your bankroll. It's going to take you, again on average, a wad of cash about as large as the royal flush itself to survive long enough to hit it.

Is a Friday paycheck starting to sound good about now?

143

DEAR MARK: *By reading your column and listening to your tapes "Hooked on Winning," you've got me trained to look for the best value on 8/5 progressive video poker machines. What are the key jackpot figures I'm looking for to at least break even against the house?* **Susan I.**

Susan, to be even against the house you need to find a machine with a progressive jackpot that is larger than 1750 maximum bets ($440 for $.05 machines, $2,200 for the $.25 machines, and $8750 for the $1 slots). Want a mathematical two percent edge? Look for jackpots of $625 on your nickel, $3,125 on the quarter, and $12,500 on the dollar machines. Tough to find, but do they exist. Good luck.

(When Susan was referring to 8/5, and I, 9/6 in the Q&A above, we meant the payoff for a full house and a flush with one coin inserted.)

DEAR MARK: *How would you go about identifying a good-paying "deuces wild" video poker machine versus a bad one?* **Angela C.**

The key to evaluating the potential return on a "deuces wild" machine, Angela, is the payoff on four-of-a-kinds. If your local casino has little competition, that hand is paid 20 for 5, rather than 25 for 5. Since four-of-a-kinds occur frequently, this lower payoff drops the percentage return by well over six percent. Some machines, though, will give you a little extra by paying more for the full house. But overall, if you're playing on a machine which pays just 20 for a four-of-a-kind, you're playing less than a full pay version of Deuces Wild.

DEAR MARK: *Is it important in video poker to play the full number of coins?* **Jerry R.**

Yes, because if you look at the paytable closely you will notice a non-symmetrical progression on the royal flush payline. Your typical royal flush payline looks like this; 250, 500, 750, 1000, 4000. Note the jump with the fifth coin inserted. Not playing that fifth coin, Jerry, will cost you 12% over the long haul.

"It is not best that we should all think alike;
it is difference of opinion that makes horse races."
– MARK TWAIN PUDD'NHEAD WILSON

♠ 73 ♠
Casinos See Raising Table Limits
as Economic Common Sense

DEAR MARK: *Last weekend, on three separate occasions, the pit boss raised the table limits higher while I was playing. It went from $5 to $10, then all the way up to $25. Why do they do that?* **Rick D.**

Given where your question came from, Joliot, my guess is that you were playing on the green felt flotillas on the river. From the casino's point of view, not mine, it makes fiscal sense to raise the limits when the boat is full of captured customers willing to surrender to higher table limits. They figure, Rick, you won't swim to shore.

Here in Nevada, many casinos have the policy of raising the table limits for new players only. Your $5 play would have been grandfathered in.

DEAR MARK: *Recently I hit a jackpot for $1,200 on a 25¢ slot machine. The casino was not going to pay me until I provided them with my drivers license and social security number. I only complied because I wanted my winnings. Was there any way around this?* **Stan G.**

Not really, Stan. Casinos are required to report to the IRS any slot jackpot of $1,200 or more. Because you played at the quarter level, your best bet would have been finding a machine that had a jackpot of $1,199—one dollar below the amount at which casinos are forced to take identification. Some exist on the boats in the midwest.

DEAR MARK: *What is the house edge in Caribbean Stud and what are my chances of being dealt a natural royal flush, straight flush, four of a kind, full house and a flush?* **Dan H.**

The game Caribbean Stud carries a 5.6 percent house edge.

The odds of hitting a royal flush are approximately 650,000-1, 70,000-1 against a straight flush and 4,000-1 against a four of a kind, 700-1 against a full house and 500-1 against a flush.

145

DEAR MARK: *Are casino owners ever afraid of system players?* **Mark J.**

Gamblers believe in systems, the casinos believe in the mathematics of the games. Most, if not all, casino owners would be willing to give away the house—room, food and beverage—to any system player willing to wager big bucks.

DEAR MARK: *In a previous column you mentioned that you didn't like Multi-Action blackjack, but you failed to give an explanation. How about one?* **Dawn G.**

Why? Because Multi-Action multiplies the urge for most players to misplay their hands.

Far too many players employ a never-bust strategy because they are afraid of losing all three bets at once. They stand on a 12 regardless of the dealer up-card. They wish, hope and pray the dealer will bust on one or more hands. This can be a bankroll-killer. At a $5 minimum table, if you are not willing to risk $15 on a hit/stand decision, you should not be playing Multi-Action.

Secondly, you blackjack bankroll has to be higher. Five dollar players have to make $15 worth of bets. A few triple losses and you're in the keno lounge begging for free drinks.

Finally, many times the house rules of Multi-Action are inferior to that of regular blackjack. An example of this would be not being able to double down after splits on a Multi-Action game.

You work hard for your money, Dawn. Why give the casino any extra edge?

♠ 74 ♠
If the Player is Wrong,
See Rule Number One

DEAR MARK: *Good-day from Melbourne, Australia. While having a surf on the internet I came across your columns and found them interesting.*

The questions you receive as a dealer took me back to what I didn't know about casinos until I started to work in one. I found some of your past columns informative about a patron's feelings towards certain situations that can be quite distressing to those uneducated in casino etiquette. Patron feelings are something we dealers tend to forget about in our very repetitious and occasionally stressful shifts.

That said, in your years of dealing roulette, did you ever have a patron that did not understand the words "no more bets," and then drop a stack of chips over the whole layout to make a reconstruction of the winning wagers more difficult (thank god for surveillance).

This happened to me today, for the first time, and all I could do was stand there with my lower jaw dropped to the table thinking obscenities I've never thought before. I was amazed, shocked, annoyed and possibly disappointed at the extreme actions of the player. Unfortunately for me the management decided it was my fault. How? That I will find out later. Any thoughts? **No identification please, for job security**

Front-line casino employees have two rules when it comes to casino patrons. One, the player is always right, and two, if the player is wrong, see rule number one. Not easy when a certain percentage of players have an attention deficit disorder in need of a Ritalin prescription. BUT, didn't you state in your question "not knowing about casinos until you started to work in one?" Like you before casino employment, inexperienced players don't know or understand casino procedures. You, in an untiring way, need to patiently explain the rules to casino guests.

147

Casinos are not in the business of harassing, then alienating, a patron for life. You will never win an argument with casino management on customer service. Their main business is to extract as much money out of the customer as possible and put a smile on his face. Not allow you to wipe the smirk of his kisser.

So unless a player is cheating the house on the roulette table—past posting, I suggest you slow down, educate new players on the proper etiquette of play and be more tolerant of unskilled patrons.

DEAR MARK: *I witnessed a rare sight at the Monte Carlo in Las Vegas this month. In a Caribbean Stud Poker hand, the player and dealer tied—they had exactly the same 5 cards. There was a minor dispute on what to do with the bet. The dealer initially ruled a push, then called over pit boss one, who agreed. Pit boss two then wandered over and declared that the player should lose because the object is to beat the dealer's hand. The player objected (he had a $25 ante and $50 on the back). Finally, a third manager was called and he declared the hand a push, returning the ante and bet back to the player. Would a certain suit rule over another in case of a tie? Also, what is the official ruling?* **Vincent K.**

No poker game, video or otherwise, is suit specific on any hand. There are machines and games that offer a special bonus for certain suited hands, but that does not affect duplicate hands on Caribbean stud poker. The correct ruling on identical hands would be a push.

Noting his mother's visit to Las Vegas the weekend before she died. "She got to go to heaven four days early."
– PRESIDENT BILL CLINTON

148

♠ 75 ♠
Rules that Improve
Blackjack Conditions

DEAR MARK: *In Atlantic City we are forced to play on a shoe (multiple-deck) game. How much of an edge am I giving up to the casino?* **Dan M.**

Compared to a single deck, a two-deck game handicaps your play - 0.35%, four decks, -0.48%, six decks, -0.54% and eight decks -0.58%.

As you can see, Dan, it is always to your advantage to play on a game that offers the fewest decks. Also note, the house edge goes up substantially when you go from one deck to two, but the change is less dramatic as you add more decks.

So how much is this costing you in dollars and cents? If you were to play 100 hands per hour at $5 per hand, each -0.1% would cost you approximately 50¢ per hour. Playing on a game with two decks versus one will cost you $1.75 per hour, with each additional deck costing you increasingly more.

DEAR MARK: *Is it better for a new player to sit on a blackjack game that has no players or one that is crowded?* **Mary Anne W.**

For all new players I recommend playing at tables with low minimum bets ($1-$2) plus play at a busy table. Besides having more fun with comrades, you will make fewer bets per hour, which decreases your exposure to the almighty house edge.

DEAR MARK: *Of all the proposition bets on a crap game, which wagers should the player avoid?* **Marty G.**

This column forever examines the making of any wager when good bets, with a lower casino advantage, also exist. So my reply, Marty, is ALL OF THEM!

Answering your question directly, the worst proposition bet on a crap game is the "any 7" bet. With this one-roll wager you win if a 7 rolls, but if any other number appears, you lose. The odds are 5-to-1 of a 7 rolling, but the casino will only pay you 4-to-1. This gives the house an edge of 16.7%. Ouch!

DEAR MARK: *Thank you for making me a smarter blackjack player. I now carry my basic strategy card whenever I play, progressively bet more when I'm winning and always set loss limits and win goals. Unfortunately, where I play, the casino doesn't offer the best playing conditions for players. What are the best rules to look for when playing black-jack?* **Stephan H.**

Smart blackjack players always play in a casino that offers the best rules. To avoid hostile playing conditions in blackjack, look for the following combination of rules that are favorable to the player:

- a single deck game
- surrender, both early and late
- double down allowed on any two cards
- double down allowed after splitting pairs
- multiple pair splitting allowed, plus resplitting aces
- dealer stands on a soft 17
- deep deck penetration

Because no two casinos are alike, Stephan, no two blackjack games are created equal. The extra effort you make finding the most favorable playing conditions will be fiscally meritorious.

DEAR MARK: *While visiting my mother in Maine, I met her neighbor who was willing to sell me a slot machine (see enclosed picture) for $700. I know nothing about the machine other than he claims it works fine. As you can see it looks in very good condition. Is it worth $700?* **Blaine G.**

Here is a simple test to tell if a slot machine is in good running order. Insert a few coins and if nothing comes out, it's working fine.

The machine in the picture you sent me is a Bally "EM" machine worth, in good condition, between $1,000 and $1,500. It is an electro-mechanical controlled slot machine, has open contact switches and was the best selling slot machine in the '60s and '70s.

Unfortunately, Blaine, you reside in Pennsylvania, where it is un-lawful to own machines built after 1941, even for private ownership. Though very reasonably priced at $700, this machine with its manufac-turing date creates a weighty legal dilemma.

♠ 76 ♠
You Won! Great. Now Pay Uncle Sam

DEAR MARK: *I was recently in Las Vegas playing roulette and came away with a large $2,000 win at Bally's. What surprised me is they didn't request filling out any information for the IRS. I have in the past won $1,300 in slots and was requested on the spot to supply the required information like SS number, driver's license, etc. for a W2-G. Why are table games treated differently from slots when it comes to gambling?* **Stan B.**

The difference between table games and slots is that when you insert three slugs and hit it big, bells ring, lights flash and a host of freeloaders climb all over your back looking for a handout—including Uncle Sam. On table games, sizable wagers of $1,300 are the norm for high rollers. Can you imagine the casino stopping a table game like blackjack every time a player wins a $1,500 hand to make the player fill out a W2-G? For this reason the IRS has Revenue Procedure 77-29, which is the guideline to gamblers for tax purposes on the treatment of both gambling winnings and losses.

Back in 1977 the IRS introduced the W2-G (statement of gambling winnings) to replace form 1099 for reporting gambling wins as well as income tax withheld. According to the IRS, the payer must issue you a W2-G form if your winnings are $600 or at least 300 times the amount wagered. This would be representative of winnings from dog racing, horse racing and state lotteries. Casino winnings are treated slightly different as a W2-G must be issued and filled out by the casino if a bingo or slot machine win is in excess of $1,200, or net proceeds from a keno win are greater than $1,500.

Note here that I stated "net proceeds" from keno being larger than $1,500. The amount of winnings can be offset by the amount wagered on your ticket for that one game. This is a benefit to keno players who mark extensive way-tickets that can cost them well over $100. Some players even play certain tickets that have payoffs of exactly $1,500, then back off the dollar they wagered, and avoid having to fill out a W2-G.

151

Oh yes, one more thing. Now that you have won a jackpot and received a W2-G, don't think there is any way of avoiding your tax bill. The IRS also receives a copy of the W2-G from the casino, and now their computers also know of your fortunate winnings.

DEAR MARK: *Is it true that a video poker machine internally knows which cards it initially deals and then gives you lousy cards so you won't have a winning hand?* **Mark S.**

Without hesitation, Mark, I unequivocally state, slot machines in regulated gaming jurisdictions have random outcomes. You can be confident that laws are in place to assure you a square game, without shenanigans.

Most states operate with gaming regulations that require their gambling devices to have a random outcome. In order to satisfy this requirement, slot machines of all types use a random number generator software algorithm to determine the games' results. This insures that all video poker machines are based completely on chance, just as if the cards were dealt from a perfectly shuffled deck. BUT, the operative phrase here is "regulated gaming jurisdictions."

Some casinos operate in locations without any forcible gaming statutes. Examples would be Indian reservations not subject to state regulations, internet casinos and cruise ships that sail in international waters. Also observe, Mark, that technology does exist so slot machines won't act randomly; instead, they are pre-programmed to avoid giving you a royal flush. These machines are illegal in Nevada, New Jersey and all states that pattern their gaming regulations after these two industry leaders. You might, nonetheless, stumble on them in ungoverned casinos.

They were burying a high-roller in Las Vegas and a few of his gambling cronies were gathered grave side when the minister said; "Gus is merely sleeping." His best friend was heard muttering: "I've got a hundred that says he's dead."

♠ 77 ♠

Same Price, Less Sauce

DEAR MARK: *I seem to be having less success playing the video poker game, Deuces Wild. I'm playing the same way I normally do. Is there something I should be on the lookout for since I play Deuces Wild exclusively?* **Sharon T.**

Sharon, let me try to make a real-life comparison here. When you go to your local grocery store to purchase a jar of spaghetti sauce, you're probably paying the same amount as you did a year ago. But look closely at the glass container. It's shrunk! Now it's a 28 oz. jar where it used to be 32 oz. The same probably holds true with the Deuces Wild machines you're playing on. You pay the same price to play it, but you're now getting less in return. Are the casinos cheating or rigging the machines so you'll lose more? Not at all. They most likely changed what they pay you for four-of-a-kind.

Expert players evaluate the potential return on a Deuces Wild video poker machine by the payoffs on four-of-a-kind hands, so in casinos with limited competition or ones tightening the screws a bit, you're normally paid 20 coins versus 25 for each coin inserted on that payoff. Because four-of-a-kinds occur frequently, this lower payout drops the percentage return by almost 6.5%.

So, Sharon, I recommend first finding, then playing, only full-pay machines, ones that give you 25 coins for each quarter played.

DEAR MARK: *A friend, who claims he knows a lot about blackjack, told me you should always split 10s when the dealer is showing a six. Does he know what he's talking about?* **Ellen G.**

This reliable source, Ellen, does he stand behind you while you're playing your hard-earned cash offering advice but never wagering his own money?

Seriously, Ellen, there is only one time when it's proper basic strategy to split 10s and that's on a face-up blackjack game. Face-up blackjack is where all the cards dealt are exposed, including both of the dealer's cards. Only here does correct strategy dictate you splitting 10s against a dealer's 13, 14, 15, 16.

But I can't recommend this version of blackjack to anyone because even when using perfect basic strategy, the casino edge is 2.0% compared to 0.4% with regular blackjack. Why 2%? Mainly because you lose when you push (tie).

DEAR MARK: *Can a greenhorn player stick to a few simple bets instead of mixing up his wagers on a crap game?* **Samuel K.**

Absolutely, and I advocate it.

When you join the euphoria of this action-packed game and give craps a try for the first time, you need not be intimidated. Just step up to the table with confidence and play these two outstanding craps wagers. A pass line bet and placing the 6 or 8. Both have a house advantage of under 1.5 percent.

A few pointers first. Ask your friendly dealer (generally the first two hours of his shift) how to make these bets. Also, look for the lowest table limit you can find, preferably $2 or less. Even with a low house edge, no need to make it an expensive learning experience. Also note here, I'm not mentioning odds. True, they are the best bet the casino offers, but, the devil is in the details. I will revisit odds in the near future when more space is available.

Finally, disregard those proposition bets (hardways, field bets, one number rolls, etc.) the dealer is barking out. Some can have a house advantage as high as 16 percent—higher than the interest on your Visa Card.

If you stick with the smart wagers I mentioned above, your liaison with the crap table should be a pleasant one.

♠ 78 ♠
You Won't Get the Shaft if
You Toss a Good Hand

DEAR MARK: *One of my greatest fears in a casino is playing over a jackpot, especially one that has a big payout like a royal flush. Does this horror story happen often? By the way, I normally play in Atlantic City.* **Thomas R.**

No cause for concern, Thomas. The New Jersey Casino Control Commission requires that all machines lock-up when the top award is hit. So if you are dealt a natural royal flush, you won't screw up and chuck those terrific cards. Which is a good thing because casinos offer free booze alongside gambling.

Additionally, all reel slot machines lock up when awards are higher than $1,200. Not because the casino wants to avoid payment and give you a blooper award instead, but because it's an IRS regulation. Uncle Sam wants his piece of the win as well.

DEAR MARK: *Is it true that the minimum required payout on slot machines in Atlantic City is 83%?* **Millie L.**

It depends on the type of slot machine that you are playing, Millie. For a pull handle slot machine, yes, it must be programmed to return "at least" 83%. But for a game of skill, like video poker, the return must be two percent higher. Why the additional two percent? Because characteristically recreational players never bother to include skill in video poker, resulting in mistakes, creating 2-4% lower paybacks. If a video poker machine was programmed to return just 83% and had a non *Deal Me In* reader playing it, the return would be less than 83%. Hence, games of skill need to return a higher percentage.

155

DEAR MARK: *In past columns you have informed your readers how to identify a good jacks-or-better video poker machine from a poor one. I exclusively play Deuces Wild. Is there a way of determining one machine from another?* **Jeff N.**

It is very simple to tell the difference between an excellent Deuces Wild paytable and an inferior one. Simply look at what you are paid for four-of-a-kind with one coin inserted. If the machine returns 5 coins, you are on a full-pay machine. By playing perfect basic strategy, your return can be 100.76%. If the video machine returns just 4 coins, your yield will be considerably lower—94.34%. It makes sense, Jeff, to always shop for value and play a premium paytable.

But also note, Jeff, theoretically, the machine is pre-programmed to return $100.76 for every hundred dollars inserted if you implore "optimum play"—that is, play every hand perfectly. Plus, "theoretically" means over the long haul, not each and every time your posterior is sitting in front of the machine.

DEAR MARK: *I have been told that there is no way of telling how much the machines return to the players on the Indian reservations in Michigan. Nor have I ever seen it advertised anywhere. Is this true?* **Jenny G.**

Yes, to a point, Jenny, that statement is correct. The Indian casinos of Michigan are not required by law to release information on their slot machine percentage paybacks. But, according to the Michigan Racing Commission, which is responsible for regulating the tribes' slot machines, the casinos must meet the same standards for machines as in New Jersey or Nevada. In New Jersey the minimum return is 83%; Nevada it's 75%. Thus, Michigan Indian casinos must return at least 75% in order to comply with the law.

But it is competition or a lack of it, not laws, that really dictates the return to patrons. All casinos in Nevada and Atlantic City return well over 90% because the competition is fierce for your greenback. The same can't be said in Michigan where the Indian casinos are spread out all over the state. Let's hope, Jenny, with the three additional casinos coming on-line in Detroit, casinos up north will start advertising payoff returns to keep current patronage.

♠ 79 ♠
Who Needs a Spleen Anyway?

DEAR MARK: *While surfing the internet I found your column on the Detroit News web page. My guess is that you must be familiar with casino gaming coming to the Motor City. Recently I have come into a small inheritance and would like to invest it in a business close to these new casinos. Any suggestions would be appreciated.* **Nathan B.**

For starters, a Cash for Gold or a pawn shop could complement gambling well. A Plasma Center would work. Oh, don't forget, Nathan, tell your customers they really don't need two kidneys.

DEAR MARK: *Could you please explain the Kelly System of betting?* **Ken W.**

Called the Kelly Criterion, it is a money management system that, at least on paper, Ken, gives you the ability to maximize your expected winnings by betting an amount that is proportional to your bankroll. By using this method a player wagers a certain percentage; example, 10% of his current total bankroll on every play. After each win or loss, you then recompute your bankroll and bet the same percentage accordingly. The biggest positive is that when you are on a losing streak, your bets become smaller and smaller, helping you avoid a gambler's meltdown. On a winning streak, your bets become larger and larger, allowing you to parlay your funds. Many gamblers find this to be a very effective systematic approach to money management.

I plan on giving the Kelly Criterion a run this college basketball season using the free picks of Roger Right (http://DealMeIn.org/roger.html). Starting with a modest bankroll of $200, I plan on wagering 15% of my current bankroll on each of Roger's picks throughout the entire season. I will let you know how it played out.

DEAR MARK: *Is there any one sure-fire way to win at the slot machines?* **Jerome C.**

Sure-fire ways, sure, I will give you three: (1.) Get a casino gaming license and operate your own slot business. (2.) Invest in the solid companies that manufacture slot machines. (3.) Buy an antique slot machine and sell it when the demand increases.

DEAR MARK: *Can I make more as a part-time gambler than I could a full-time teacher?* **Susie H.**

Taking into consideration the importance and magnitude of your job, the time, the effort and commitment, yes, even a losing campaign as a part-time gambler probably pays better.

I would not be the first, Susie, and hopefully not the last to say that you are both underpaid and undervalued in your honored profession.

DEAR MARK: *When is the best time to surrender in blackjack?* **Tom H.**

When surrendering in blackjack, Tom, you give up half your wager for the privilege of not playing out your hand. Known as one of the more sophisticated moves in blackjack, surrendering is best utilized when the dealer is showing a 10 or ace and you have a hard 15 or 16. This particular hand will lose more than three out of four times as opposed to you only losing half you bet. If your favorite casino allows surrendering in the above scenario, wave the white flag.

DEAR MARK: *Playing craps with a pass line bet and a point of 9, I asked the dealer what were my chances of winning. He said 40%. Was he right?* **Janice G.**

Janice, the dealer was correct when he told you 40% with this simple formula illustrating it. There are six ways a 7 will appear (3-4, 4-3, 5-2, 2-5, 6-1, 1-6), and four ways a 9 can show (5-4, 4-5, 6-3, 3-6). Obviously, one of these ten combinations must happen for your bet to be decided. So, because, on average, you'll make the point of 9 four of ten times, there's your 40%.

♠ 80 ♠
How the House Makes its Bread on the Spread

DEAR MARK: *How does a casino make money on sporting bets when you bet against the spread?* **Nick L.**

Whenever you place a point-spread type wager, Nick, you lay 11 to win 10. That means if you want to win $100, you have to wager $110 no matter which team you are betting. If you win, you will collect $210— your $110 wager plus the $100 you just won. This commission, also called a vigorish (a.k.a. vig), is the compensation taken by the house on every sport bet wagered.

DEAR MARK: *My brother-in-law never makes a bet on his favorite football team, but on the final score. What type of bet is that?* **Cindy H.**

Football betting, Cindy, offers you the ability to wager on the combined total of points scored by both teams during a game. This bet is called a "totals" wager or an under/over bet. Winning an over bet requires that more points be scored than the linemaker's total. Winning an under wager requires that fewer points be scored.

DEAR MARK: *What percentage of sports bets do I have to win to be even against the casino?* **Jessup C.**

To break even against the house edge, you need to win at least 52.38 percent of any point-spread wagers you make.

DEAR MARK: *In our office football pool, I place near the bottom almost every week. Any advice on what I can blame my continuous losses on?* **Randy V.**

Sports betting is a combination of both skill and luck. Your wins, Randy, come from your superb handicapping skills. Just blame your losses on a late game interception or fumble.

DEAR MARK: *What is your longest winning streak betting sports?* **Matt O.**

I once developed rotator cuff tendonitis patting myself on the back when I picked winners in 19 out of 20 horse races over two days when my ponies either won, or placed, at Del Mar. Also, I have done extremely well handicapping the Indianapolis 500. Other than that I feel I'm like the veteran losing gambler who was hopelessly hooked on football betting. Nothing else interested him. Unfortunately, he lost almost every bet he made. Finally, even his bookie felt bad for him. "You lose all your bets," said the bookie. "Why don't you bet on hockey instead of football?"

"Hockey" said the gambler in dismay. "But I don't know anything about hockey!"

DEAR MARK: *I live in California and don't want to drive to Las Vegas just to place football bets. I've heard that you can make wagers to sportsbooks in Nevada over the phone. Any truth to this?* **Russell M.**

Nevada casinos do offer account wagering via the phone, Russell, but ONLY if you live in the state of Nevada. Making a bet from outside of Nevada violates the Interstate Wire Act (18 U.S.C. 1084). This code provides criminal penalties to anyone engaging in the business of betting when using a wire communication facility for the transmission of interstate (that's you, Russell) or foreign commerce of bets or wagers on any sporting event or contest. Russell, you technically can't even call up a high school buddy who is dealing dice at the Mirage and ask him to place bets for you.

DEAR MARK: *I realize that I am betting a long shot when I bet a 10-team parlay, but what are my true chances of hitting it?* **Lorenzo D.**

The casino will pay you 500 for 1 when you hit a 10-team parlay, but your chances of hitting one are 1,023 to 1. Ouch! Too sweet a profit for the casino for my hard-earned money.

♠ 81 ♠
Nothing is a Sure Bet in a Casino, but Streaks Sure Help

DEAR MARK: *In roulette, if red came up five times in a row, would you advise switching over to the black since streaks do not last forever?* **Al M.**

One thing a player who has been around gambling for any length of time knows is that the streaks can and will happen. It is one of the many life lessons you learn in the casino. Gambling, like life, is loaded with streaks. Many gamblers bet streaks so they won't get emotionally involved in bucking a trend. And when you are on one, oh the joys of telling your friends and family.

But along with the above advice comes this caveat. For a gambling analogy, note the agate type at the bottom of a mutual-fund advertisement. "Past performance is no guarantee of future results." In other words, just because red appeared five times in a row, that does not mean it will happen again. Assuming you are playing on an unbiased wheel, the ball has no memory, and red can appear again or not for the next 20 spins.

DEAR MARK: *NASCAR is one of the fastest growing spectator sports. We can bet on football, baseball and basketball, but how about betting my favorite driver, Jeff Gordon, to win?* **Jimmy B.**

You can bet Jeff's #24 Dupont car not only to win, but to place or show. Also available are quinellas, exactas and even some prop bets. My personal favorite is betting individual drivers against each other. An example of this would be Geoff Bodine in the QVC Ford finishing higher in the race standings than Ward Burton's MBNA Pontiac. The reason I love this wager is not my knowledge of the sport, the drivers or the teams, but some sports books post the odds prior to the finish of Saturday's time trials. Then they don't change them. For those of us, Jimmy, who follow racing, this can be a license to print money.

Gentleman, start your wagers.

DEAR MARK: *I have been told that before putting your first coin in a video poker machine, it already knows what hand you will be dealt. True or false?* **Denise C.**

Video poker machines work like this, Denise. When they are sitting in an idle mode, the machine is constantly crunching numbers waiting for the next sucker—I mean gambler. When a participant walks over and inserts a coin the machine is triggered into knowing it has a live gambler on the hook. The random number generator (RGN) crunching numbers stops, then picks the combination of cards you will see on the screen.

DEAR MARK: *I have an amusing (at least to me) anecdote about losing in a casino. I had been playing blackjack and lost about $400. I then went up to my room and my wife asked me to get her a soda. I went down the hall to the soda machine and inserted my dollar. The machine wouldn't give me a soda or my money back. I was grumbling about this all the way down to the hotel's convenience store until I realized I was more upset about that one dollar than all the money I had lost all day.*

Now here's my question for you: Does the casino have more than a 2% advantage on the soda machine? **Andrew R.**

Haven't you heard the saying, Andrew? "Change is inevitable, except from a vending machine." Actually, I would guesstimate your average vending machine holds about 8%, the same as poor play on a blackjack table.

"Stop cheating!" the dealer told the card player.
"I'm not!" claimed the player.
"You must be," said the dealer.
"That is not the hand that I dealt you."

♠ 82 ♠
Tabasco Style Blackjack

DEAR MARK: *I recently came across a blackjack game called Spanish 21. I didn't play but the rules looked very similar to regular 21. Any differences before I give it a try?* **Seth G.**

There are two notable exceptions when comparing Spanish 21 to a regular blackjack game. In Spanish 21, all the 10s (not the Jacks, Queens, Kings) are removed from the deck. Also, the player gets paid for a hand total of 21, or the standard three-to-two payoff for a blackjack, even if the dealer's hand is a natural blackjack. Additional player friendly rules are; doubling down on two or more cards, pair splitting and double downs up to four times after splits, bonus payoffs for different combination 21s, and a super bonus that pays out $1,000 for a suited 7-7-7 when the dealer's up card is a seven. (Side note: In my entire 18-year gambling career I've never seen this occur, whether dealing or observing countless hands of regular blackjack as a pitboss.)

So, Seth, even without the 10s in the deck, is Spanish 21 a good play? Yes, if you utilize perfect basic strategy. By employing Spanish 21 basic strategy—which obviously differs from normal blackjack strategy—you reduce the house edge down to .8 percent. Deviate and the house advantage can be up to three percent.

DEAR MARK: *I am a keno writer who works in Las Vegas. One of our regular customers asked if I knew how many different number combinations are possible in keno. I told him "in the thousands" but I wasn't sure. How many possibilities are there?* **Diane S.**

You were off, Diane, a few quintillion. To be exact, there are 3, 535, 316, 142, 212, 174, 320 numerical combinations using 20 balls with 80 numbers to choose from.

163

DEAR MARK: *In Las Vegas a few casinos now offer 100X odds on a crap game. What is the house advantage on this bet?* **Tim T.**

The house edge is 0.09%. As minuscule as this is, Tim, you better be capitalized to the hilt before you embrace this wager. Two or three seven-out, line away calls and you're in the poorhouse.

DEAR MARK: *If my playing style in blackjack does not give me a positive result in computer simulations, will it still help me win in actual casino gambling?* **Felix S.**

The only playing method that will give you a positive expectation in blackjack is card counting. Period!

DEAR MARK: *What I like best about craps, besides winning, is how much fun it is. Why don't more players enjoy playing the game?* **Ernie M.**

You are correct, Ernie, craps is fun, craps is social, craps is exciting, but except for an odds wager, all craps bets come at a cost. Craps is a negative expectation game, meaning that no matter how you bet, the odds are against you.

I recommend all players treating craps like a bag of M&Ms. Eat (bet) only the colors (pass line, place bets) you like (a wager with a low house edge).

DEAR MARK: *I heard it is a felony to cheat in a casino in Nevada, even at a $5 blackjack game. True?* **Kenneth K.**

Be it $5 or $5,000, cheating in a casino is a felony punishable by up to 10 years in a rudimentary Nevada hostel—prison. Cheating is one mistake that a misinformed player who romantically envisions himself as a cagey cat should avoid. Most, if not all, casinos will prosecute to the full extent of the law.

♠ 83 ♠
One Taco Short of a Combination Plate

DEAR MARK: *In all your years in the casino industry, I bet you never heard of this type of superstitious gambling. My brother-in-law brings a small computer to his hotel room that has a software program that tracks a person's biorhythms. He then proceeds to ask dealers their birth dates, runs back up to his hotel room, then plots the dealers' emotional, physical and mental state. Then he goes back to the casino and only plays on a dealer's table if the software shows a dealer in a down cycle. Beat that!* **James M.**

You would think, James, that after 18 years in the business I would have seen enough to have seen too much. Then you come along with your brother-in-law's nincompoop gambling theories.

My personal favorite was when a lady playing on my blackjack game pulled out a Ken doll dressed in black and whites that even had a bow tie duplicating the one I was wearing. After every hand I (the house) won, she inserted straight pins into my likeness and started a voodoo conversation with the doll. Here is proof that evolution CAN devolve.

I believe that your brother-in-law, and others who gamble with insane beliefs in the paranormal, are a few Fruit Loops shy of a full bowl.

DEAR MARK: *Recently my wife won $1,125 on a slot machine and a few hours later, in the same casino, I won $1,260. I'm not complaining, but why did they ask me for my social security number and have me fill out forms and not ask my wife to do this?* **Gary R.**

165

Because your jackpot total was in excess of $1,200. Anything above that and the casino reports your winnings to the IRS. You can, however, offset the taxes by reporting your losses if you keep good records. Don't despair if you didn't; that is, if you use a slot club card. Because your play is tracked, the casino should be able to provide you documentation regarding the machines you have played and how much you've previously lost.

DEAR MARK: *Another gaming columnist recently advised a reader that splitting 10s is always appropriate when the dealer's up card is a 5 or 6. He was using the advice of author John Scarne. You, on the other hand, recommend never splitting 10s in the standard version of blackjack. Whose advice is right?* **Bill S.**

Actually, I received this question via a telephone call from Bill, as we both live in northern Nevada and had access to the same column. I must say, I, like Bill, was surprised that the columnist used John Scarne as his point of reference for blackjack hitting rules.

John Scarne's book, *Scarne on Cards*, was first published in 1949, well before computers could analyze blackjack with multi-million hand simulations. Consequently, since 1962 when Edward Thorp, the first blackjack specialist using a computer (IBM 704), published his book *Beat the Dealer*, no blackjack author recommends splitting 10s—under any circumstances. Scarne stands alone.

Also, since our conversation, I took Bill's question one step further and ran a 20 million hand simulation test using a piece of software called BJ Trainer. The results clearly favored leaving those 10s alone versus splitting them against a 5 or 6.

Should a computer be trusted over a highly acclaimed author like Scarne? Not always. I don't have a baseball bat alongside my computers ready to inflict a mortal wound for nothing. But for crunching numbers to compare the variables of blackjack, I'm in favor of using computer results over advice written in 1949.

> *"You cannot beat a roulette table unless you steal money from it."* – ALBERT EINSTEIN

♠ 84 ♠
The Kid Wasn't Ready Yet

DEAR MARK: *My spouse and I have a dinner riding on your response. Because we live in a very small town with limited video rentals, we need an answer from you to the following question. I say the Cincinnati Kid lost his final wager in the movie of the same name. My husband believes he won and became the reigning poker player of New Orleans. Who is right?* **Lou J.**

The Cincinnati Kid's (Steve McQueen) full house of Aces and 10s was no match for the straight flush, eight through queen of diamonds, that Lancey (Edward G. Robinson) had.

The Kid: "I'll call your five thousand and raise what I have in front of me."

Lancey: "Call your thirty-five hundred and raise you five thousand."

Great dialog and suspense at the end but by poker playing standards, Lancey, by raising, then trying to draw to an inside straight flush, would be ridiculed today by even the most amateur poker player. He should have folded. But as Lancey said, "It gets down to what it's all about. Making the wrong move at the right time."

Incidentally, the final wager was not at the poker table but pitching pennies with a local shoe-shine boy. "The Kid" lost that bet also. "You try too hard, man" said the shoe-shine boy. "You just ain't ready for me yet."

Maybe you can squeeze two dinners out of your husband. Enjoy your night out, Lou.

DEAR MARK: *In Montreal, the dealer gets only one card on the deal. Does this change that delicate balance of the game, particularly when you are on third base sitting with a hard 16 and looking at a dealer's up card of 10?* **Tom M.**

Nay, Tom. The main reason the dealer receives just one card is strictly for casino security.

Dealing one card averts both the unscrupulous dealer from tipping off customers to their hole card, or when checking the ten/ace, inadvertently flashing what's hiding in the hole to an over-observant card sharpie.

DEAR MARK: *For someone learning card counting strategies in blackjack, what do you feel will be the greatest obstacle I will encounter?* **Jan S.**

As you didn't identify yourself coming from either Wall Street or WalMart America, let's put aside the pitfalls of being under-capitalized.

The greatest obstacle when making frequent, multiple, table-limit bets is that your play will be closely monitored. First, plan on the eye-in-the-sky (observation) analyzing your play. When casino security assesses that your biggest wagers always correspond with higher counts, believe me, you'll feel the heat of a camera over your shoulder. If the trend continues, the phone ringing in the pit will be about you, not who the pit boss likes in tonight's Red Wing/Flyer game. Finally, a decision will be made about your play. Yes, the death blow. A polite banishment to nickel slots. It generally goes like this: "Hi, Jan. You're just too good for us. You're welcome to play any of the other games we offer but we don't want your action in blackjack."

To avoid exile, Jan, you will need to learn how to conceal your high-count bets without using so much camouflage that you will counteract your advantage.

DEAR MARK: *I know you can bet on the horses, but can you bet on motorsports in Nevada? I would really have liked to place a bet on my favorite driver in the recent Daytona 500.* **Dave D.**

Quick rule of thumb, Dave. If a professional sporting event is preceded by the national anthem, by golly, you can get action on it in the Silver State. Besides major racing events like the Daytona or Indianapolis 500, many sportsbooks will take wagers on the whole NASCAR and CART season.

By the way, Dave, this ditty crossed my desk from a reader this week. I thought, you having the same passion for auto racing as I, might enjoy it.

"Race fans, I had inferred from my one trip to the Brickyard 400, fell into one of two categories: tattooed, shirtless, sewer-mouthed drunks, and their husbands." Steve Ruchin of Sports Illustrated.

♠ 85 ♠
Three's a Charm

DEAR MARK: *My favorite number is three. I was born on 3/3/1933. I regularly bet three on the roulette table, make $33 dollar wagers in blackjack and always play the third machine from the left on a slot carousel. Over the years it has paid decent dividends. Is there such a thing as a lucky number?* **Freddy G.**

Lucky charms, shooting stars and special numbers, all are performance poetry, mystical rituals that give the illusion of hope. Your belief that your number is lucky, Freddy, is a way of asking fate for a favor. Because three out of four adults have at least one lucky charm or ceremonial offering (mine is picking up pennies with heads up), who am I to argue?

The number three has been considered the luckiest number for thousands of years in cultures and religions all over the world. "Of all the numbers in the infinite scale none has been more universally revered than three," writes Philip Waterman in *The Story of Superstition.* Christianity and the Trinity, China's third day of a new moon, Egypt's three-sided pyramids, the list goes on.

In casino action, I've seen players stand up from a blackjack game, turn around three times to reverse their luck, then proceed to pulverize the house.

So, does the number three have any supernatural powers that work like a charm? Well, it does remind me of an old horse bettor's joke: "A guy wakes up at 3:33 a.m. one morning and takes the number three as an omen. He gets into a taxicab numbered 333. He goes to the track and bets $333 to "win" on the third horse in the third race...and true to form...the horse comes in third."

169

DEAR MARK: *Every time I touch my money in the betting circle on a blackjack game, the dealer starts yelling at me. Why does he have to make a federal case out of it?* **Kristi A.**

I learned the hard way that a dealer's job, first and foremost, is game protection. Repercussion: a week on the streets. I had a terrible habit of turning my back on the table layout to chit-chat with whomever. Eventually Guerrilla military training "Avoid game security being broached at all costs" was close-order drilled in to my finite brain cells.

The casino's anxiety is the deceptive player who "pinches" or "caps" his wager. Pinching is when a card sharp tries to remove chips or money from a losing wager just before the dealer seizes losing bets. Capping is just the opposite of pinching. Here the player has an excellent hand against the dealer's up-card and wants to add more chips to his wager.

DEAR MARK: *In Atlantic City, they do not offer a Big 6 & 8 bet like they do in Nevada. Are we being ripped off here on the east coast?* **Alex G.**

Quite the contrary, Alex. Thank your state legislature for having the foresight to eliminate the 6 & 8 from the crap layout through gaming statutes. By betting the Big 6 or 8, you are paid even money by the casino. Bet $6, win $6. This gives the house a whopping nine percent edge over a Big 6 or 8 wager. By asking the dealer to "place" the wager instead, the casino edge is reduced to 1.515% percent. You are betting the same $6, but your "friendly dealer" will pay you $7 for the exact same wager.

"A dollar picked up in the road is more satisfaction to us than the $99 which we had to work for, and the money won at Faro or in the stock market snuggles into our hearts in the same way."
– MARK TWAIN

♠ 86 ♠
Consider Tipping a Contribution
to the Dame of Fortune

DEAR MARK: *Does tipping in any way affect your chances of winning in a casino? Also, do you know where tipping originated?* **Emilee D.**

Technically tipping does not influence a player's winning destiny, but gratuity is always in good form and helps keep up the morale at the table. Look at tipping, Emilee, as a donation to "Lady Luck." *(Biased thoughts from someone—that would be me—who was a longtime compensation for service employee.)*

The custom of tipping has its roots in England more than 200 years ago. Samuel Johnson is given credit for establishing the tradition that has evolved into the present-day tip. In the 18th century London coffee houses, Johnson and his friends would hand their server a slip of paper with coins attached. On the paper was written, "**T**o **I**nsure **P**romptness." The acronym of this phrase is apparently the derivative of the word "tip."

DEAR MARK: *What was the largest bet ever made on the Superbowl?* **Donna D.**

The largest "legal" wager ever made was an 8 to 1 money line bet (the outcome of a game without points) that San Francisco would beat San Diego in Superbowl XXIX. An unidentified gambler wagered $2.4 million at the Mirage in Las Vegas. The 49ers won big and the gamester collected $300,000.

DEAR MARK: *What are the odds of hitting a hole-in-one in golf?* **Sam S.**

According to the Professional Golfers Association (PGA), custodian of statistics on such matters, a male professional's or a top amateur player's chances are 3,708 to 1; a female pro's odds are 4,648 to 1. The average duffer's odds are 42,952 to 1.

My lone ace, when I teed off from the eighth hole and it landed in the cup on the 12th green, probably wouldn't count.

171

DEAR MARK: *After many years of playing video poker, I have noticed that I end up with an excessive amount of hands that make up a single pair. I realize that some pay (jacks or better), but most don't. Am I getting too many or my fair share of pairs?* **Ken Y.**

A disproportionate amount? Not at all, Ken. The probability of a single pair materializing is 42.26 percent. Combinatorial mathematics tells us that a 52-card deck generates 2,598,960 unique five-card hands, of which 1,098,240 hands can make up any one pair.

DEAR MARK: *What is a "buy" bet in craps, how does it differ from a "place" bet and what are the payoffs of each wager?* **Hank M.**

In lieu of waiting for a number to show up as your point for a pass line bet, you may "place" or "buy" that number. Both work but are not paid the same way. By placing or buying a number, you are wagering that your number will roll before a 7.

Place bets on the 4 or 10 are paid 9-5 for a house edge of 6.67 percent, the 5 and 9 are paid at 7-5 (4 percent edge) and the 6 and 8 at 7-6 for a 1.52 percent house advantage. Buy bets work the same as place bets, except that you must pay a 5 percent commission to the house on all buy wagers. In return, the casino will pay you at true odds.

Because the house edge is less than 5 percent when placing the 5, 6, 8 and 9, it's not worth buying those numbers. True, buying the 4 or 10 can reduce the house edge to 4.76 percent, less than if you were to place them; still, the price is too egregious.

Buy, place, commissions, true odds, yes, Hank, it can be complicated, but here is my one bet recommendation: "Place" only the 6 or 8. Lose the rest from your betting arsenal.

♠ 87 ♠
Substantiating Your Losses
a Must with Uncle Sam

DEAR MARK: *You said on slot winnings more than $1,200, the dreaded IRS form must be completed. Having never won a jackpot of this size before until recently at Stateline, NV, I am confused. It took that much of my money to win that jackpot. How can I offset the tax due on my win with my losses?* **Lucille O.**

You can offset your gambling losses against your winning jackpot on Schedule A as an Other Miscellaneous Deduction, but only to the extent of your gambling win, not your income from a 9-to-5 job. Gambling winnings are reported on tax form 1040 on the Other Income Line. Reportable gambling winnings include lotteries, bingo, raffles, horse and dog racing and all casino games, legal or otherwise. Yes, even an illegal bet on Denver in the Superbowl can be considered a gaming win, or if you wagered on Atlanta, a deduction.

Also, Lucille, you must be able to substantiate your losses with flawless documentation. How? By supporting your losses with a descriptive gambling diary. You do this by keeping track of all wagering tickets, canceled checks, bank withdrawal statements made at the casino and credit receipts as your proof. Granted it is impractical to record every pull of the handle, but by keeping a daily log of where you played, how much you gambled and how much you won or lost will be acceptable evidence for substantiating your triumphs and tolls of gambling.

By the fact that you have never won a big jackpot before, I infer that you probably did not keep factual gambling records of your slot play. Don't despair; that is, if you use a slot club card. Most casinos use some form of computerized tracking system similar to the one called the SMART system (Slot Marketing and Revenue Tracking System) that IGT provides the casinos. With these Smart systems, the casino records your detailed playing history. Because your play is tracked electronically when using a slot club card, the casino should be able to provide you with the documentation needed to corroborate your losses.

One final thought, Lucille. Don't just get your recorded play at the casino where you hit it big. Go back to the other casinos where you have used a slot club card and ask for a printout of all your play on their machines for that year. I state "that year," as gambling losses can be used only to counterbalance gambling winnings during that same tax period. They cannot be carried forward or back to any other tax year.

DEAR MARK: *I love to play Nevada Megabucks but can't afford $3 every pull. Occasionally I try to second guess the machine's rhythm of hot and cold cycles and play accordingly. Obviously that means playing less than $3 each time. Is this a bad strategy?* **Rob S.**

With all my parochial schooling, Rob, I always thought the rhythm method had something to do with birth control.

No progressive machine, Rob, should ever be played without the maximum amount of coins required. With all progressives, a percentage of all coins played goes into the progressive jackpot that continually grows until some lucky soul hits it. But if you don't play the maximum amount of coins, you can't retire from your crummy job. Your jackpot with one coin inserted would be a picayune $5,000—not enough to tell your boss to "shove it." I suggest you look at a progressive meter and consider what a nincompoop you would be if you lined up the three Megabucks' symbols but failed to risk two additional tokens.

"A lottery is a salutary instrument and a tax...laid on the willing only, that is to say, on those who can risk the price of a ticket without sensible injury, for the possibility of a higher prize."
— THOMAS JEFFERSON

174

♠ 88 ♠
The Secret to Video Poker

DEAR MARK: *If dealt A, K, Q, J, of hearts and a 10 of diamonds on a video poker machine, should I try for the royal flush or stick with the straight? This happened to me recently and I kept the straight, kicking myself ever since. How bad a move was it?* **Patricia M.**

Stop kicking yourself, Patricia, but you did mess up.

When playing video poker, all experts will discard certain cards to optimize the "expected value" (win potential) of their hands. Herein lies the secret to winning at video poker—or another way of saying it, playing perfect basic strategy.

So what do I mean by "expected value?" Expected value is the average value of all the wins attainable (after the discards are replaced), assuming that the optimum cards are retained and each unique possible draw occurs. In your case, the Expected Value of a 4-Card Royal was 19 and straight is just a 4.

By now, Patricia, I suspect you think this expected value stuff isn't worth learning since I've mentioned previously that there are 2,459,076 possible hands you can be dealt in video poker. Not necessarily. In reality, there are only 35 workable combination of hands, from the naturally dealt royal flush to that crummy hand where you would discard all five cards. learn them and you'll lower the house edge to under one half of one percent.

My only solution at this time, Patricia, is to tell you that every hand you are dealt has some value and potential of winning money, with the expected value predetermined accurately by past computer studies. Hopefully by summers end I'll be bringing those computer studies to a four color, laminated chart form, which will identify each of those 35 combinations. I'll make sure you, and all the readers of this column, know when it's available.

DEAR MARK: *I want to make some decent sized wagers (10-20K) on a few games this upcoming football season. Ideally, I would like to make them in Vegas, but that is not really practical for me. I know there are various internet off-shore books who will take bets via bank wire and telephone. I am willing to risk the legal implications of this, 18 USC 1084 notwithstanding, but I am worried about wiring $20,000 out of the country to some guy I've never met except for 3 minutes on the telephone.*

Do you know which of these telebet books are reputable? Or not reputable? And how much do they generally take in wagers? Is $20,000 a great deal to them? Any information that you care to share would be greatly appreciated. Thanks. **Arnold J.**

Arnold, didn't you answer your own question when you stated "I am worried about wiring $20,000 out of the country to some guy I've never met except for 3 minutes on the telephone?" I think you summed up your potential risk quite well. Besides, as a syndicated columnist, it wouldn't be appropriate for me to dole out illegal advice on how to best beat the Interstate Wire Act.

Finally, I've mentioned this once before in a previous column, but I can't advise anyone to wire money thousands of miles away to an unregulated, uncontrolled, and probably illegal enterprise, give them a credit card and social security number, and hope everything is square.

Sorry, Arnold, no vote of confidence here.

"Never play cards with a man called Doc."– NELSON ALGREN

♠ 89 ♠
Waiving the White Flag in Roulette

DEAR MARK: *I was playing roulette and betting on the outside in a Missouri casino. Double zero hit and I lost my whole bet. I asked why I didn't get half my bet back as I thought was the rule, but the roulette dealer had no idea what I was talking about. Was I wrong or is this just a Missouri rule?* **Darren D.**

The croupier in Missouri would not have known what you're speaking of because only Atlantic City, by law, offers a "surrender" rule on all even-money outside bets on the roulette layout.

Because there are no single zero wheels in Jersey, all Atlantic City casinos feature double zero wheels that have both 0 and 00. If you bet black or red, 1 to 18 or 19 to 36, or odd or even, and the ball lands on 0 or 00, you only lose one half of your original wager. This is known as the "surrender" rule and it cuts the casino edge in half from 5.26% to 2.63%. The surrender rule only applies to these even-money bets. For all remaining wagers the casino edge remains a hefty 5.26%.

DEAR MARK: *Can you explain why casinos have similar atmospheres? The lighting and sound seem to create a certain ambience conducive to gambling, or am I imagining this?* **April F.**

Bullseye, April. Most of what you see, feel and hear in a casino is methodically and deliberately arranged to separate you from your money as painlessly as possible.

DEAR MARK: *Why is it that certain slot machines never pay off?* **Dina S.**

All slot machines, Dina, consistently pay. They pay the casino's rent, the light bills, and all the employee's salaries. They also pay millions of dollars in profits to casino owners and stockholders. The player just so happens to be on the low end of the food chain.

DEAR MARK: *Do you have a favorite video poker paytable (machine) that you like to play?* **Peter T.**

Unfortunately, Peter, you won't encounter my favorite video poker machine in your gaming jurisdiction, Missouri. They are even difficult to find here in Nevada. But when you do, you are playing on one of the best video poker machines available. It is a Jacks-or Better machine with a 10/7 paytable. With perfect basic strategy, it returns, over the long haul, 101.94% to the player. Use a slot club card that offers generous cash rebates and the machine will yield well over 105% against the house.

DEAR MARK: *What do you mean by a kicker in video poker?* **Mavis K.**

A kicker is a single card held with a pair. For example 7, 7, A or Q, Q, K are hands in which an extra card (the kicker) is retained.

When playing kitchen table poker it is okay to hold a kicker in certain scenarios but never in video poker. Kickers add absolutely no value to a video poker hand.

DEAR MARK: *Exactly what is Crapless Craps? Also, is it worth playing?* **Pete N.**

Also known as Never Ever Craps, Crapless Craps is another example of a casino offering that could cost you dearly if you belly up to a crapless crap table.

In this modified variation of a regular crap game, you can't lose on the come out roll if the shooter tosses a 2, 3 or 12. Instead, it automatically becomes the point, just like the 4, 5, 6, 8, 9 and 10 on a standard game. You also don't win if the shooter throws a natural 11. It too becomes the point. With these additional funky rules, the house now holds a 5.4% edge on your pass line bet versus 1.4% on a typical crap game.

Ho-hum games or wagers won't cut it here, Pete. Crapless Craps rates a "no play" for *Deal Me In* readers.

♠ 90 ♠
Who's Watching Whom in the Pit

DEAR MARK: *What is the power structure of the casino pit and how far did you rise? Also, whose job is it to observe that no one is cheating?* **Paul D.**

The pecking order is as follows: dealer, boxman, floorman, pit boss, games shift manager, casino shift manager and finally casino manager. My hierarchical assault up the ladder ceased at the casino shift manager's position—held for such a brief period you could time it with a stopwatch—because I incessantly broke rule number one of casino advancement. NEVER MAKE SUGGESTIONS! Besides, I spent an inordinate amount of time in my gaming career on secret-double probation.

As for cheating, reverse the chain of command. The casino manager watches the shift manager, who watches the pit bosses, who watches the floorman, who watches the dealers—with the eye in the sky (cameras in the ceiling) watching everybody.

DEAR MARK: *What is the worst move a player can make with a dealt hand in blackjack?* **Becky L.**

Getting ridiculous here, Becky, it's actions like doubling down on a natural blackjack. I've seen this happen once with a $200 wager when alcohol got the best of this party animal. But for the average player it's standing on a pair of eights against the dealer's upcard of 7. Instead, you should split those eights. A player making this basic strategy error will lose 70 percent of the time.

DEAR MARK: *When in Las Vegas, my mother-in-law plays a certain combination of bets that she believes are better than other wagers on a roulette table. You said that all bets on roulette have the same house advantage with the exception of one. Who's, and which bet is it?* **Judith C.**

Most players mistakenly believe that certain wagers on a roulette table are superior to others. Example: Playing the even money bets (red/black or odd/even) are always better plays than wagering a straight-up number. Nothing could be further from the truth. All bets, with the exception of one, hold the same house edge of 5.26%. That one wager is the five-number bet, 0, 00, 1, 2, 3—also called "the beast with five numbers." Makes sense, as the house advantage on this sole wager is 7.89%.

It behooves your mother-in-law, Judith, on her next trip to Las Vegas, to play the more advantageous European, single zero wheel at the Monte Carlo, Stratosphere or a few of the grind joints downtown. The house edge on a single zero game is reduced to only 2.7%. That's shopping for value or *Deal Me In* gambling.

DEAR MARK: *What is the most superstitious bet players make on a crap game?* **Bill C.**

When the dice fly off the table, superstitious players call off respectable working wagers and start betting the next roll will be a seven. Betting like this is why your simplex gambler always loses to Joe casino owner. By believing in superstitions, naive players attempt to predict the individual and unpredictable roll of the dice. The casino owner only concerns himself with the quite predictable return on each and every wager.

In the case of possessed betting that the seven will appear, the house has a 16.1% edge.

DEAR MARK: *For us non-card counting players, why is it more important to find single deck blackjack games?* **Sunny R.**

Because blackjacks, which pay 3 for 2, occur more frequently on a single deck versus multi-deck games. Example: Let's say, Sunny, your first card is an Ace. On a single deck game, 16 of the remaining 51 cards, or 31.37 percent, are the face or 10-value cards that would complete your blackjack. On an six-deck game, 96 of the remaining 311 cards, or 30.87 percent, would give you your snapper.

♠ 91 ♠
Treat All Winnings as
YOUR Hard-Earned Money

DEAR MARK: *My friend believes I have a problem gambling with money that I win. She says I treat it as "the house's money" and continue to play till I lose. Is she right?* **Norma B.**

Nowhere is it written—in the U.S. Constitution, the Talmud or the Nevada Revised Statutes—that the money you win at any neon carpet joint is still the property of the casino. Treat all winnings, Norma, as YOUR hard-earned money.

DEAR MARK: *Why does my husband sneer at my slot play? This from someone who loses a whole lot more at the crap table.* **Mary P.**

Even though many table game players look down on slot players, take heart, Mary, and please share this gambling yarn with your spouse.

There once was a crap shooter whose wife, a slot player, approached her spouse on a crap game informing him that she needed more money to play slots. "What happened to the $100 I gave you?" he asked? When she replied, "I lost it," he criticized her for playing slots. "Well I've been playing for three hours and I'm having lots of fun," she said. "You've been playing craps for three hours. How much have you lost?"

"I'm down a few thousand," he said, "but I know how to gamble!"

DEAR MARK: *Our senior citizen's group is being offered a great deal on a bus trip to Atlantic City. Not only do we get a buffet but also $20 in quarters. The problem is that I am a small-time bettor who prefers nickel slot machines. I have been told that none exist in Atlantic City. Any suggestions for us conservative gamblers after our $20 is gone?* **Betty K.**

Nickel machines are an industry staple here in Nevada, but unfortunately Atlantic City is one tough market for the low roller. It seems only "The Donald" (Trump) feels the low-limit customer is of any value. I suggest you convert your quarters to nickels and play at either Trump Marina, Trump Plaza or the Trump Taj Mahal.

Get there early, Betty, as the seats are always filled by cautious gamblers. The Trump Marina has only 44 nickel machines, the Plaza 274 and the Taj Mahal 141. Expect an average return of 86.8 percent.

DEAR MARK: *Is there a difference between Gambler's Ruin and Gambler's Fallacy? If there is, which affects the gambler more?* **Norm S.**

They are completely different, Norm. Gambler's Ruin is the chance of losing all of a stated sum of money, given a known statistical advantage or disadvantage on each bet, while attempting to win a stated sum. Gambler's Fallacy is the belief that the law of large numbers also applies to small numbers.

Unless you are a mathematician calculating the chance of Gambler's Ruin with decimal point arithmetic, the latter, Gambler's Fallacy, applies more to the average gambler.

Most players challenge Gambler's Fallacy erroneously believing that a sequence of events in a random process—the spin of a roulette wheel—will represent the essential characteristics of long-term play even when the sequence is short. Say black appears nine times in a row; many gamblers will now wager heavily on red because it's way overdue.

But just because you have a deviation in one direction (Black, B, B, B, B, B, B, B, B) doesn't mean an aberration in the opposite direction will occur over the short run to restore balance. Deviations are not 'corrected' as time goes on, just diluted.

The solution to Gambler's Fallacy is to treat each spin as an independent event. The roulette ball has no memory of any past actions.

♠ 92 ♠
With the Wise Guys Gone,
Wall Street Rolled in

DEAR MARK: *Is it true that the reason Caesar's treats the customer so well is because it is one of the last casinos still owned by the Mafia? Just curious because I love that place, even when I lose.* **Chris K.**

Sorry, Chris, "The Family" doesn't own Caesars, but you can own a piece of the joint, even without Italian lineage. It trades on the NYSE as ITT. The present ITT Corp. is three publicly traded entities, which brings their hotel/leisure, gaming and entertainment business together under the name ITT Corp. ITT Corp's gaming operations consist principally of Caesar's World, ITT Sheraton's Desert Inn Resort and Casino in Las Vegas and ITT Sheraton Casino in Tunica, Mississippi.

In the past, Chris, the underworld did have involvement with certain casino operations in Las Vegas. Today, because of strong state gaming regulations and the active participation of public corporations, the last remnants of direct organized crime in the gaming industry are long gone.

DEAR MARK: *Though the amount was not substantial (25¢), I believe a roulette dealer intentionally took my chip off the winning number. Then what started out as a disagreement escalated into a huge argument with both the dealer and the pit boss. To cool me down the pit boss agreed to call the eye-in-the-sky. He came back and said the dealer was not in error and I did not have any money on the winning number. Because I've been playing that same number for over 20 years, I still believe I was right and demanded to see the film. I was refused.*

I would first like to know what disciplinary action should be taken against a dealer if I was correct? Also, don't I have a right, on demand, to view the video tape? **Jack M.**

183

As you noted in your question that the amount was insignificant, here's how it should have been handled. Casino security should bury the dealer in a shallow grave and then casino management fire him for "No Call, No Show."

Come on, Jack, we're talking an $8.75 payout here. Plus, dealers can, and do, make mistakes. I've made plenty, once involving a $7,000 overpayment. Aided by surveillance film, the casino got its money back and I received a non-paid week on the streets to think about it. I took advantage of the imposed mini-vacation by spring skiing and taking part in late night revelry for seven days.

But your question deserves a sober answer; you do have the following option in a casino controversy. Here in Nevada, if you are dissatisfied with a decision made by casino management, you may appeal to the Enforcement Division of the Nevada Gaming Control Board. Enforcement agents will review the video tape, if it exists, and inform the casino and the player of their decision.

There is a reason, Jack, why most casinos are averse to showing patrons video tape of any casino activity. Cheaters have been known to make false claims over small amounts of money just to dispute a payoff and then demand a viewing of the film. The charlatan is really trying to observe the kind of surveillance coverage that the casino has on a particular game.

DEAR MARK: *Do casinos have shills at the dollar machines?* **Andy A.**

A shill, or game starter, is an individual employed by the casino to induce gambling on table games, not slots, that are being underplayed. The only place you would find a shill today is in high-limit gaming pits.

"A gambler with a system must be, to a greater or lesser extent, insane." – GEORGE AUGUSTUS SALA, ENGLISH WRITER AND JOURNALIST

♠ 93 ♠
The Law of 250

DEAR MARK: *I agree with you about judging casinos in your column "The Good, the Bad and the Ugly." I would like to add the Soaring Eagle Casino of Mt. Pleasant, Michigan to your ugly list. Besides employees being extremely rude, they charge for drinks while you're playing slots and their machines are the tightest I've ever played. If they don't change their ways soon, they're going to lose a lot of customers when the new casinos in Detroit are built. You need to let your readers know how bad it is. In the future I'm going elsewhere to do my gaming.* **Rick J.**

DEAR MARK: *What really annoys me about Casino Niagara are the high minimums on the Blackjack tables. If you are lucky you may find a few $5 tables, but the majority are either $10 or $25 minimums. I know that you preach always betting within your limits, but let's face it, for this area, it is ridiculous.*

To me, it is blatant robbery of people who like to do some recreational gaming. I don't know many individuals who can afford $25 a pop at blackjack. **Joe M.**

DEAR MARK: *Just writing to inform you that little has changed since you blasted Casino Windsor in your column, "The Good, the Bad and the Ugly." Just try getting on a low limit blackjack table on the weekends. Don't they get it?* **Robert L.**

No, they don't GET IT. The above three samplings of carpetbaggers at work proves that when a self-contained casino complex has zippo competition, you the customer are the victim of a holdup. Sure, casino operators come to town drunk with virtue on how they boost employment roles and stimulate the economy—an argument I'll debate with them inebriated or sober—but what they really have is an exclusive license to print money.

The three letters above also prove casino management has no conception of Girard's Law of 250. Girard is Joe Girard, who has twelve times been named "The World's Greatest Salesman" by the Guinness Book of World Records. The Law of 250 is Girard's belief that everyone knows 250 people in his or her life important enough to invite to a wedding or who will show up at their funeral. Mistreat one, and 250 will eventually know about it. He also believes that customers are the most important asset in the world to someone involved in sales. And casinos are selling, selling gambling.

The mentioned casinos should soul search and question if our three letter writers have already told 250 people. Can they afford to have clientele leave sore and unsatisfied? Can they afford to jeopardize the patronage of any customer, even the low roller? Worst case scenario: Disgruntled patrons might tell me, and I'll take those pillaging casinos to task in the dozens of newspapers that this column appears in across the country.

The bottom line: it's only through established competition that payouts on all games become more liberal. It's your choice; continue getting mugged or "just say no" to gambling in these joints.

DEAR MARK: *I recently saw a video poker game that drew cards from five different decks. The top jackpot at the time was $223,500. Do you know anything about this game?* **Janice J.**

Called Five Deck Frenzy, this game has earned a following among video poker enthusiasts who enjoy the super jackpot produced by the game's use of five independent decks of cards. With random card delivery, the game also provides more winning combinations than standard video poker. Marketed jointly between Shuffle Master and IGT, it uses IGT's MegaJackpot format, a wide area progressive system that offers a progressive jackpot starting at $200,000. The top hand possible in the game—five aces of spades.

Though casinos can offer video poker jackpots starting at $200,000, the probability of hitting five aces of spades is 14,896,150 to one. Hit five bullets in another suit and the jackpot drops down to $2,500.

Also note, Janice, you can't dash out and buy a new Ferrari if you achieve gaming immortality. IGT primary jackpots are paid in annual installments.

♠ 94 ♠
Bring Your Kids–Sort Of

DEAR MARK: *I wish I had read a past column you wrote called Split Decision before I made a recent trip with my family to Las Vegas. I was appalled at the amount of handbills advertising sex being pushed down my throat on the Strip right in front of the MGM Grand. Who in their right mind would bring a family to Las Vegas?* **Clifford M.**

As a result of continual complaints from tourists like you, Clifford, the Clark County Commission recently approved a ban on the passing out of handbills in Las Vegas. The ban is targeted primarily at the aggressive peddlers (smutters) on the Las Vegas Strip who force-feed fliers, most of which contain sexually explicit ads for call girl services, on unwilling tourists as they stroll by. The ban also affects businesses that hand out ads in front of their stores along the strip.

Those needing their carnal obsessions attended to in Sin City will still find arousal circulars at newspaper stands—which are exempt, as are non-commercial enterprises.

By the way, Clifford, since when is Las Vegas for those in their right mind?

DEAR MARK: *My boyfriend and I are planning an upcoming gambling trip to Las Vegas. I want to prove to my fiancee that I know a little more about chance than he thinks. Is there any even money bet in Nevada?* **Sandra R.**

Oh yeah, Sandra. Drive over to one of the 34 wedding chapels in Vegas and get married. Marriage today is statistically a fifty/fifty proposition that you'll end up divorced. And if you divorce rich—jackpot. There's your even money bet.

DEAR MARK: *Before going to the casino I run practice hands on the kitchen table. The problem with this method is that play in a casino on both video poker machines and blackjack is much faster. Any suggestions?* **Tammy D.**

The best way to acquire gaming skills without the expense of a live game is with a computer. In many ways a computer can be far superior to a human instructor for both training and drilling. The benefit of computer training is the ability to test card counting strategies along with money-management progressive win formulas at no financial risk, even with simulated high speed play. Whether at high speeds or a live game pace, computers accumulate data for later review. This will enable you to spot costly trends that you might be making on a video poker machine or blackjack table. Information like this would take you years to accumulate dealing hand after hand on your kitchen table. And again, the key here is that any knowledge obtained without a casino outlay will make you more money down the road.

Many of the better gaming software programs are either free or shareware, making it very inexpensive, easy to use, and yes, definitely fun. These software programs can be downloaded from any of the major online services on the internet.

If you don't have a computer, you can still create a Las Vegas experience with a handheld video game. I've seen these small hand-held computer games at Wal Mart's as inexpensively as $5. I prefer the games made by a company called Radica. The screen is easy to read and the batteries last, well, I've never changed them yet. Along with a basic strategy card, you'll sharpen your playing skills and be an expert in no time.

DEAR MARK: *Per your advice, my sister and I on our monthly trips to Las Vegas always discuss the games we will be playing and the correct bets to make on those games. When my sister hits the front door though, she gambles on a whim and becomes her own worst enemy. Is my sister different from most who gamble?* **Sally O.**

Take counsel, Sally, most gamblers devise a cleaver scheme to keep the casinos at bay, but like Penelope, wife of Odysseus, they spend all day weaving a tapestry of words and all night unraveling it.

♠ 95 ♠
Are Birthday Numbers
Really Luckier?

DEAR MARK: *In a past column you stated that you only play the lottery when the jackpot approaches true odds plus playing quick-pick (random) numbers. I can see your first point, but I, like most people, play my family's birthday numbers because of the luck factor. What is wrong with that?*

Also, you used the odds of hitting a California 6/51 ticket as an example. Our state lottery has 54 numbers. What are the chances of hitting it? **Dale G.**

The most popular method used by players for the selection of lottery numbers is calendar dates such as birthdays or anniversaries.

More than 65% of the tickets played in state lotteries have numbers all marked under 31. By eliminating numbers above 31, two problems emerge.

First, there is a much greater chance of sharing the bootie because such a high percentage of people, like yourself, play this way. It is odd, Dale, to have only one winner when all the numbers picked are under 31.

Second, track your state lottery draws and note how often just the numbers 1-31 occur. Fortunately for you, I did the homework by researching every draw of every game ever played in California. Even to my surprise, a ticket limiting the numbers between 1-31 appears, on average, only 3.5 times a year (104 games per year—Wednesday and Saturday draws).

So for the above two reasons, Dale, I subjectively recommend random numbers, in addition to waiting for the lottery to get close to true odds.

For your second question, I list the staggering chance of hitting the Illinois lottery (6 out of 54) below, plus additional state lottery games, indexed in ascending order of difficulty.

6 out of 25	1 chance in 177,100
6 out of 30	1 chance in 593,775
6 out of 33	1 chance in 1,107,568
6 out of 36	1 chance in 1,947,792
6 out of 39	1 chance in 3,262,623
6 out of 40	1 chance in 3,838,380
6 out of 41	1 chance in 4,496,388
6 out of 42	1 chance in 5,245,786
6 out of 44	1 chance in 7,059,052
6 out of 46	1 chance in 9,366,819
6 out of 47	1 chance in 10,737,573
6 out of 48	1 chance in 12,271,512
6 out of 49	1 chance in 13,983,816
6 out of 50	1 chance in 15, 890,700
6 out of 51	1 chance in 18, 009,460
6 out of 54	1 chance in 25,827,165

Powerball (5 out of 45 + 1 out of 45) 1 chance in 55 million.

DEAR MARK: *Can you bet either the presidential elections or the Oscars in Nevada?* **Cliff D.**

Not anymore, Cliff. Though you'll see odds posted by Las Vegas bookmakers in nationwide newspapers, they're more for amusement, not actual wagering. The Nevada Gaming Commission halted those intriguing side wagers years ago after bets like "Who Shot JR" were made by insiders knowing the eventual outcome.

That's too bad. Just think of the possibilities a sportsbook operator could offer. Like if Geraldo Rivera mentions on his talk show that he's a former lawyer, bet six to win five. Or that he finished 13th out of 364 in his law school class; here you might get 20 to one. Then there's Rivera's evening talk show counterpart, Larry King. That he's from Brooklyn and people from Brooklyn are special—even money. Or that he and his guest "go way back." Lay 10 to win five.

♠ 96 ♠
Slots Simplified

DEAR MARK: *KISS, keep it simple stupid. That's how I gamble by playing only slot machines. Can you share some simple tips on the easiest game to play, slots?* **Sherry B.**

Sherry, you're right, no great mystery here. Slots are the easiest game to play in the casino. Insert a coin, pull the handle, then reach into your purse for more money. Unfortunately, that's what normally happens when the house has such an enormous built-in edge. But that doesn't mean you can't at least close the gap against you and throw in some fun to boot. So, Sherry, below are some of my favorite slot tips to help you overcome this huge house advantage. These tips won't guarantee that you'll become an instant winner, because it's tough to beat a house edge that generally runs well over 10 percent, but it also doesn't have to be so tough on your bankroll. Let's get started.

1. The only true skill to playing slots is machine identification. Example: progressive machines offer the opportunity to compare and shop around for the best value. One 25 cent "slot machine carousel" can have a progressive jackpot of $2600 and another bank of machines—exactly the same and standing side by side—$1900. You should always be looking for the best slot opportunities possible.

2. Casinos will advertise machines that have a 98.5 percent payback. WOW! A casino game holding just a percent and a half, and on a slot machine no less. But there's a downside. If you look closely at the advertisement, it will probably say, "on select machines." Furthermore, it probably won't be posted on the machine itself, and generally will be limited to a single bank of machines in the casino. Now it becomes your responsibility to find them. Easiest way; Ask a slot employee, and if he or she doesn't know, have one of them ask a direct supervisor.

3. Las Vegas gives away over one-half billion dollars in comps each year, and as a slot player, you deserve your share. Repeat, you deserve your share. How? Casinos now offer you the ability to "comp yourself" by using one of their player's club slot cards. It's generally based on the number of coins you cycle through a machine, so you might as well get credit for all those quarters you're inserting. Shop casinos for comp value and find out what you're worth to them.

4 You always want to treat "comps" as a form of profit, but you never want to gamble just to receive them. It's much better to play a 98 percent payback machine and increase your winning opportunities than play machines with a poor return that cycle more of your coins. Remember, you're there to stay in action and possibly win, not lose your bankroll for a free buffet.

5. If you can't afford to play the maximum amount of coins, you shouldn't be playing that denomination of machine. If dollar slots are too rich for your blood, drop down to a quarter machine. It's always better value to play five quarters versus one dollar, or five nickels instead of one quarter.

6. I recommend not playing back the credits you've accumulated. Cash out and take stock. The problem with playing back credits is that the longer you stay, the machines built-in advantage eats away at them. It doesn't take long to zero out.

7. Avoid restaurant, bar, supermarket and airport slot machines. Notorious for being tight.

8. Can't decide which type of slot machine to play? If you're going to choose between video poker and slots, play video poker. Even poor play on a video poker machine will have a better payback than most "reel" slot machines.

9. Before you walk away from a machine, don't forget to press the cash-out button. Millions are lost each year by gamblers forgetting their winnings (stored credits).

10. It is your responsibility if destiny favors you that you receive full payment when hitting a jackpot. Even with some relatively small jackpots, if the slot is short coins in the hopper, you'll receive only a partial cash payment in the tray, with the balance to be paid by a slot attendant. If you were to insert more coins and pull the handle, say bye-bye to the remainder of your jackpot.

11. Read all the posted material on a slot machine. It is your responsibility to fully understand all printed information concerning the number of coins to insert, lines needed to be lit, prizes or awards. In most cases, when someone calls a slot attendant over and complains the machine "just ripped me off," that individual generally didn't read the pay schedule correctly.

12. When you insert coins, don't assume all the tokens register before you pull the handle. Played five but only four recorded? SORRY. You'll get a sympathetic pat on the back from the casino, but no money.

13. I recommend avoiding machines that use video representations of symbols. With these slots, there is absolutely no way to figure out what the payoff percentage of that machine is. For all you know, your true chances of hitting a major jackpot could be 2,097,152 to 1.

14. Most casinos will hold a slot for you while you go to the restroom, take a short break, or even go on a buffet run. Just ask a slot supervisor to reserve your machine and give a specific time when you'll return.

15. Don't chain yourself to a cold machine, even if it's your favorite. Why? Because the longer you stay on any slot, the more time the machine's built-in mathematical advantage has to work you over. This is how casinos build mega-resorts. Time always working on their side and a mathematical edge on each and every slot.

16. Just because you're only playing slots you still need to set a loss limit on your bankroll for both your trip and each individual gaming session. Divvy up your wad per playing session, discipline yourself and stick to it.

17. I'll come clean here. I don't play slots. But as a local in a casino town, I know where the locals who do play find the most cluck-for-the-buck. Simply put, locals don't play dog machines. So when searching for high payback machines, ask a few employees where the locals find the best slot value. Even if they're not slot players themselves, they at least know where their friends like to play.

18. Leave both your credit and bank teller cards at home so you will not be tempted with the easy convenience of getting cash. Also, allow me to take the obvious one step further. Only bet what you can afford to lose.

Finally, going to slot heaven—Las Vegas? Your best return in Las Vegas, and the country for that matter, are in the casinos downtown. Average return on quarter machines: 95.5 percent. That almost makes it a decent wager. Good luck, Sherry.

♠ 97 ♠
Viva Las Vegas

Before I Deal: I receive an abundance of mail from individuals making their first pilgrimage to Las Vegas asking me this or that about the gaming Meca of the world. Not one to hold back expressing my biased opinion, I will advise you that discounting 50% of my dogma would be appropriate. Two reasons why. First, I don't reside there (I live in northern Nevada but visit Las Vegas a dozen times a year) and second, I'm a journalist. Properly forewarned, here is a sampling of the many questions I get weekly.

...I'm doing a report for school... Here are some Las Vegas fun facts.
• More than 30 million people will visit Las Vegas in 1996.
• 80,000 couples tied the knot there last year.
• Las Vegas has more than 105,000 hotel rooms and is growing hourly.
• Hotel occupancy averages more than 92% annually.
• Las Vegas has 13 of the 15 largest hotels in the world.
• The average annual temperature is 66 degrees.
• The average daily humidity is 30%.
• More than 1.4 million people call Las Vegas home.
• 850 flights a day bring in more than 2.5 million visitors a month.
• MaCarren airport is the 8th busiest in the world.
• The Circus Circus buffet cattle-feeds more than 12,000 customers per day—that's four million per year.

...cheapest place to stay... In your car. A bargain compared to the Ladd Hotel back in 1905. One dollar bought weary travelers—same sex— eight hours sleep in a shared bed.

Honestly, it's a tough call because room rates change with the wind. The best time of the year though is pre-Yuletide. Between Thanksgiving and Christmas rooms can be had for under $20.

...best buffet... Here are my three favorites for those interested in abdominal distention. The Rio Buffet, Fiesta's Festival Buffet and the Texas Station's Market Street.

Warning! For the gastronomically fit.

...I collect war memorabilia from pawn shops... You mean the best place to hock your wedding ring? Try Super Pawn.

...decent steak-and-eggs special... You can't beat the $2.99 special at the Rio or the midnight breakfast specials at Binion's.

...any culture in Las Vegas... The Holyfield/Tyson fight doesn't count? Unfortunately, the only thing I do culturally in LV is walk past the exact replica of David at Caesar's Palace on the way to a hot crap table. Standing 18 feet high and weighing more than nine tons, the stone came from the same quarry in Carrera, Italy that Michangelo used to carve his David.

...best escort service... Ask the wrong person and you'll find out. The Las Vegas Metro Police Vice Squad. Avoid the breakfast they serve. Runny scrambled eggs and cold hashbrowns.

...sound guidance for a newcomer... This cautionary advice comes from Ed Reid and Ovid Demaris in, *The Truth about Las Vegas:* "The surest way to beat Las Vegas is to get off the plane that has taken you there and walk straight into the propeller."

...favorite swimming pools... The fountain at Caesar's with Giovanni Bologna's Rape of the Sabines in it. I'm not recommending this swimming hole because it will save you a trip to the Palazzo Vecchio in Florence, Italy. No, no. It's because the wishful sometimes throw in five-dollar chips for luck.

...I want to get married quickly... Try the Little White Chapel. Couples in a rush can use the drive-through window.

...best hamburger... Those with cholesterol levels below 250, try LJ's Place. Above 250, get your doctor's permission.

...best place to shoot pool... The Lion's Den. Forget the fact that it's one of the largest pool halls in the world, or that it is new and clean. I like it because it has straight pool sticks.

...I love singing at Karaoke bars... You're kidding, right?

...looking for a good Sunday brunch... The Sunday brunch in the Ti Amo at the Santa Fe is the best 10 dollars you'll ever spend in Nevada. An incredible value for the price.

...any good prime rib specials... The 16-ounce slab at the Lady Luck for $6.99 is pretty hard to beat.

...looking to waste some time... Check into the 5,005 room MGM Grand Hotel and try to find your way out.

...easy way to get a comp for a low roller... Head to Vacation Village and buy in for $10 in nickels at the video poker bar. You'll instantly become a high roller by receiving a free hot dog and beer.

...best Mexican food... The Tex Mex at Z Tejas is hot, hot, hot.

...cheap beer for the non-player... Seventy-five cents for a Corona, Becks or a Heineken equals a cheap buzz in my book. Slots A Fun, the little annex next to the Circus Circus, serves up some of the cheapest brew in town.

...best hot dog... Las Vegas is home of the 99¢ foot-long hot dog. Journey down the strip and you can easily eat your weight in wieners. But I ask you, is there a better hot dog than Nathan's of NY? New York, New York has them. Case closed.

...I want to get away for the day... From neon to nature, I highly recommend hiking or mountain biking in Red Rock Canyon. Red Rock Canyon's enormous scarlet silence will overwhelm you like nothing manmade can.

...most overrated attraction... Once is enough for the Mirage volcano, but nothing can touch the Freemont Experience downtown.

... things to do in Las Vegas for children... Wet 'N Wild is my kid's favorite, but better yet, get in your car and take I-15 west five hours to Disneyland.

...biggest Free attraction... A battle between the crew of the Britannia and a hearty gang of pirates from the Hispaniola every 90 minutes, for five minutes, is decent. As they say: "To the victors go the spoils of Treasure Island." Just like the casinos, the pirates always win.

...easiest way to get your hands on some real money... While you are downtown, stop by the Binion's Horseshoe from 4 PM - Midnight for a free souvenir photograph next to one hundred $10,000 bills. I'll wager that Benny Binion made that million dollars over and over again from the inquisitive wandering in for the free photo.

♠ 98 ♠
Salvo Cannonade of Craps Questions

Before I Deal: Craps can be mind-boggling entertainment, making mince-meat out of those who don't understand the fundamentals. My guess is that fewer than one percent of players truly grasp dice. The only thing greener than the felt on your typical crap game is not the money won, but the players. What proves my one percent theory is that on any crap game, most, if not all, players make at least one wager that has a house advantage of between 6-16 plus percent. But if you've read my column long enough, you know that I feel any wager, on any game, with a house edge in excess of 2%, is a SUCKER bet.

Anyhow, questions on craps continue to be numero uno in subject matter received, so I decided to shorten, and answer, some of those pesky little buggers collecting dust on my desk.

What is better, placing the 6 or 8 or betting on the Big 6/Big 8? **Kenny W.**

It's exactly the same wager BUT the Big 6 and 8 pays even money, whereas placing the 6 and 8 pays 7 to 6. House advantage on the Big 6 or 8 is 9.1%. Placing the 6 or 8 has only a 1.5% house edge. Eliminate the former from your betting repertoire.

Are the bets the stick man recommends good wagers? **Chris A.**

NO! Repeat, NO! The suggested wagers the stick man is barking—field, hardway and craps wagers—all own a high house advantage. These bets should be limited to the tootsie pop crowd—a.k.a., the sucker born every minute club.

What is the difference between a throw and a roll? **Larry I.**

A throw is one roll of the dice. A roll is a series of rolls until a decision (seven or the point) is made.

Can I remove my bet before the next throw? **Martha M.**

Any bet can be removed from the table with the exception of a pass line or come line wager if the point has been established.

197

What is a Horn-High Eleven Bet? **Bob. T**

A one roll wager, the Horn-High Eleven is a five unit bet; one unit on the number two, one on three, one on 12 and two units on 11. Sucker bet.

Is there any absolute way to beat the game of craps? **Jerry H.**

Absolute way? Absolutely. DON'T PLAY.

Should I place all the numbers? **Randy T.**

Only place the six and eight. The 4 and 10 have a house advantage of 6.7%. The 5 and 9 is 4.0%. And what are they, Randy? Sucker bets.

What is the difference between 5 to 1 and 5 for 1? **Susan L.**

5 "for" 1 returns five units, whereas 5 "to" 1 returns six units on working wagers.

How many different possible rolls of the dice are there and which number appears the most? **Cheryl. G.**

There are 36 possible combinations with the seven coming up six different ways, or 16.67% of the time.

Name all the wagers on a crap game that have less than a two percent house advantage? **Becky C.**

Pass line, don't pass, come line, don't come, odds and placing the six and eight.

The best bet on a craps game is? **Larry V.**

Odds on your pass or come line bet. House edge—ZIPPO.

Should I ever place a wager on the pass line after a point has been established? **Mark B.**

Never. At this point the house has a much bigger edge because the point has been established. On the come-out roll you need those sevens and elevens to maintain that low house edge of 1.41% on a pass line bet.

Can I sit down and play craps? **Bobby C.**

Generally no, unless you're blessed with Saudi Arabian oil wealth or a high roller of the same magnitude.

What is a call bet? **David L.**

A voice bet, acknowledged by the stickman, without chips on the selection.

What did the dealer mean when she asked me if I wanted to "press" my bet? **Shirley M.**

To increase or double your previous wager and return any excess winnings to you.

I found a 25 cent crap game in Las Vegas. Can I just bet 25 cents on the pass line? **Brian M.**

Generally, yes, and you still get free cocktails to boot. Some casinos may request a 50 cent minimum wager.

How many throws of the dice occur on an active game per hour? **James M.**

Good dealers can push the dice well over 200 times per hour, making craps the most consistent live action game the casino offers.

Can I request my place bet to be working when the point marker (puck) is marked off? **Robert A.**

Yes, but you must inform the dealer that you want your bet working.

What do the two dice signifying 12 on the Don't Come or Don't Pass line mean? **Ronald M.**

It means if the 12 rolls, it's a tie. You neither win nor lose.

Why are odds and place bets generally "off" on the come out roll? **Jay M.**

To avoid confusion. Besides, you're rooting for the seven to roll for your new pass line bet.

♠ 99 ♠
The Side of Gambling
Casinos Seldom Talk About

DEAR MARK: *I am a graduate student working on my Masters degree in Abnormal Psychology. My thesis is on Compulsive/Problem Gamblers. Any information on the extent of the problem, trends, profiles and treatment of problem gambling would be greatly appreciated.* **Jane B.**

I questioned myself, Jane, if your inquiry was appropriate for this type of column—unequivocally YES!

Extent of the Problem: The magnitude of problem gambling ceaselessly draws heated debate. Groups like the National Coalition against Legalized Gambling believe the wrath of gambling leads to the gates of prison, insanity or death. The casino industry disputes any figure and gives problem gambling limited lip service. Setting biased opinions aside, a good frame of reference is the number of studies showing that anywhere from 5-10 million people in the United States (2% of the population) can be considered compulsive gamblers, with an additional 3% problem gamblers. Research also indicates that as many as 7% of teenagers could be addicted to gambling.

Trends: As gambling proliferates across America—legal in 27 states by 1998—one frightening trend always, repeat always, appears. Saturate any area with gambling and the prevalence of problem gambling spirals upward. I am personally inclined to believe that problem gambling will continue to accelerate north for two reasons.

1. Social attitudes toward gambling have changed from negative to positive.

2. Church and state got into the gambling business. Be it church bingo, Las Vegas Nights, the lottery or casino gambling, both institutions not only legitimized gambling but depend on these legalized activities as a way of generating revenues.

Profile: Until the mid-1970s, your typical compulsive gambler was a white, middle-aged man. Today's profile according to the Council of Compulsive Gambling of New Jersey crosses all ages, races, religious persuasions, socioeconomic levels and educational lines. Below is their snapshot of your typical compulsive gambler.

• Nine out of 10 problem gamblers are men.

• 91% of problem gamblers who paid off their gambling losses continue to gamble.

• 17% attempt suicide.

• 96% began gambling before the age of 14.

• Three out of 4 compulsive gamblers commit felonies because of gambling.

Treatment: What works? Gamblers Anonymous. Gamblers Anonymous offers the following questions as self evaluation. These questions are provided to help the individual decide if he or she is a compulsive gambler and wants to stop gambling. Most compulsive gamblers will answer yes to at least seven of these questions.

1. Did you every lose time from work or school due to gambling?
2. Has gambling ever made your home life unhappy?
3. Did gambling affect your reputation?
4. Have you ever felt remorse after gambling?
5. Did you ever gamble to get money with which to pay debts or otherwise solve financial difficulties?
6. Did gambling cause a decrease in your ambition or efficiency?
7. After losing did you feel you must return as soon as possible and win back your losses?
8. After a win did you have a strong urge to return and win more?
9. Did you often gamble until your last dollar was gone?
10. Did you ever borrow to finance your gambling?
11. Have you ever sold anything to finance gambling?
12. Were you reluctant to use "gambling money" for normal expenditures?
13. Did gambling make you careless of the welfare of your family?
14. Did you ever gamble longer than you had planned?
15. Have you ever gambled to escape worry or trouble?

16. Have you ever committed, or considered committing, an illegal act to finance gambling?

17. Did gambling cause you to have difficulty in sleeping?

18. Do arguments, disappointments or frustrations create within you an urge to gamble?

19. Did you ever have an urge to celebrate any good fortune by a few hours of gambling?

20. Have you ever considered self destruction as a result of your gambling?

For my loyal readers: Bet with your head, not over it. If you or someone you care about has a gambling problem and wants help, call GAMBLERS ANONYMOUS.

GAMBLERS ANONYMOUS is a fellowship of men and women who share their experience, strength and hope with each other so they may solve their common problem and help others recover from a gambling addiction. The only requirement for membership is a desire to stop gambling. For further information write or call:

Gamblers Anonymous

International Service Office

P.O. Box 17173

Los Angeles, CA 90017

(213) 386-8789

(213) 386-0030 fax

http://www.gamblersanonymous.org

isomain@gamblersanonymous.org

♠ 100 ♠
Sometimes You Wonder
Who Runs the Nut House

DEAR MARK: *I have heard that in some casinos in Las Vegas a pit boss will keep track of a dealer's gains and losses on a per shift basis, and the subsequent pit that they get assigned to will be based on these numbers. Generally speaking, hot dealers (dealers who are winning more than they are losing) will be assigned the higher limit tables. Two different dealers in one casino told me how much pressure they were under to win. Is this true?* **Darrell L.**

If it is, Darrell, you've got dimwits running the insane asylum. Dealers assigned to the high-limit table games should be those with both experience and the ability to deal to heavy action without feeling the pressure of the dollar denomination. Unfortunately, some pit supervisors sweat the money as if it were their own pirated loot and have been known to take the casino's losses out on your friendly dealer. Quoting Forest Gump: "Stupid is as stupid does."

Funny thing, Darrell, deep down, casino management knows the money, over time, will always swing back the casino's way regardless of the dealer's flaming wizardry. It is too bad that in some casinos heat from management is still part of a dealer's job description.

Over the long haul, the "hot" dealer for any casino is a dealer who can deal the most hands per hour. Period! If I ran the asylum, give me a dealer who can pitch plus pay and take with speed, not one who charts out having the hot hand that day.

203

DEAR MARK: *How do the dealers like the Shufflemaster and does it speed up the game?* **Joe L.**

Speaking as a former dealer, most of us dislike shuffling machines. Shuffling allows the dealer to catch his or her breath, plus it breaks up the monotony of only pitching cards. Now, speaking with my former casino management suit on, we love the Shufflemaster because we can grind out more hands per hour on a game that has a built-in house advantage.

DEAR MARK: *Are progressive slot machines programmed to hit different with the amount of coins played? I have been told that the jackpot hits more often with one coin played. Yes or No?* **Gene A.**

Gene, you've got to start reading this column more often. I have answered your question one way or another at least six times this past year.

The definitive, absolute, conclusive answer is NO. A jackpot will not hit more often if you play fewer coins.

DEAR MARK: *Because a royal flush is really only a straight flush with a fancy name (as well as the highest straight flush), why then is it more powerful than five-of-a-kind or deuces wild?* **Dan H.**

When was the last time you hit a royal flush, Dan? I know plenty of video poker players who never have. The odds of hitting a royal flush are almost 40,000 to one.

A five-of-a-kind hand uses four additional wild cards (deuces), making the hand relatively easy to obtain. On a deuces wild paytable, five of a kind ranks fourth behind a royal flush, four deuces and a wild royal flush. You should be able to hit one by your second roll of quarters. A royal flush can be elusive your entire lifetime.

"If I had the money and the drinking capacity, I'd probably live at a roulette table and let my life go to hell." – MICHAEL VENTURA

♠ 101 ♠
Acquire Skills at Home Before You Expose Your Hard Earned Money

DEAR MARK: *Before going to the casino I run practice hands on the kitchen table. The problem with this method is that video poker and blackjack machines play much faster. Any suggestions?* **Tammy D.**

The best way to acquire gaming skills without the expense of a live game is with a computer. In many ways a computer can be far superior to a human instructor for both training and drilling.

The benefit of computer training is the ability to test card counting strategies along with money-management progressive win formulas at no financial risk, even with simulated high speed play. Whether at high speeds or a live game pace, computers accumulate data for later review. This will enable you to spot costly trends that you might be making on a video poker or blackjack machine. Information like this would take you years to accumulate dealing hand after hand on your kitchen table. And again, Tammy, the key here is that any knowledge obtained without a casino outlay will make you more money down the road.

Many of the better gaming software programs are either free or shareware, making it very inexpensive, easy to use, and yes, definitely fun. These software programs can be downloaded from any of the major online services on the internet.

If you don't have a computer, Tammy, you can still create a Las Vegas experience with a handheld video game. I've seen these small hand-held computer games at Wal Mart's as inexpensively as $5. I prefer the games made by a company called Radica. The screen is easy to read and the batteries last, well, I've never changed them yet.

Along with a perfect basic strategy card, you'll sharpen your playing skills and be an expert in no time.

DEAR MARK: *I was wondering if you knew the name of the guy who came to Vegas with a couple hundred bucks and kept winning millions. He said, "I'm going to win the casino." I believe this happened at Binion's and as the story goes he ended up broke. Do you know where I can get more info?* **Brian F.**

Which loser are you talking about? There are hundreds of riches to rags stories that litter Interstate 15 as you're leaving Las Vegas. Sure, a few players arrive in a Gremlin and drive home in a $250,000 vehicle, but it's generally a Greyhound bus. Your typical mere mortal ends up going to the casino gift shop and buys a tacky t-shirt that says, "I'm Here Visiting My Money In Las Vegas."

The only way a player can guarantee making a small fortune in Las Vegas is to arrive with a large one.

DEAR MARK: *Why are the table felts blue in Morocco?* **Darren S.**

Because green is the sacred color of Islam; also known as the "Color of the Prophet."

DEAR MARK: *Years ago I was told by an instructor at William and Mary that the university was partially funded by the lottery. Was he pulling my leg?* **Shelly D.**

No he wasn't, Shelly. William and Mary as well as Yale, Harvard, Dartmouth, Brown, and Columbia were funded by voluntary taxation (lottery).

DEAR MARK: *How can the casino afford to give away a 99¢ breakfast?* **Tom D.**

Because they wish, hope and pray that you'll spend $200.99 before you leave.

DEAR MARK: *I'm curious, when you worked in a casino, what was the most often asked question players asked you then?* **Gail S.**

Where's the bathroom?

♠ Notes ♠

♠ Notes ♠

♠ Notes ♠

♠ Notes ♠